THE HOLDING SKY OF AWARENESS

EXPERIENCING JOY THROUGH EGO DIS-IDENTIFICATION

by

TODD J. LYON, M.D.

authorHOUSE®

AuthorHouse™
1663 Liberty Drive, Suite 200
Bloomington, IN 47403
www.authorhouse.com
Phone: 1-800-839-8640

First published by AuthorHouse   10/11/2007

ISBN: 978-1-4343-2669-0 (sc)

Printed in the United States of America
Bloomington, Indiana

This book is printed on acid-free paper.

CONTENTS

ACKNOWLEDGMENTS

I have experienced tremendous support and assistance during the creation of this book. I am deeply grateful to so many.

To Steve Ford who has never doubted and always supported this work. Thanks for your many useful suggestions and, mostly, for the gift of your friendship that, like fine wine, has ripened with time.

To Tom Pratt and Robin Bruck for their enthusiasm and encouragement. Thank you for opening to and sharing with me during a difficult time.

To Michele Denman for her ongoing support for this work. Your excitement for this work has renewed me many times.

To Michael Kimball for his expertise and experience in the worlds of writing and publishing. Thanks for unselfishly sharing your time and knowledge with me.

To Doug Williams and John Van Ness for their thoughtful consideration of this work. Thank you both for supporting this process and your many helpful suggestions.

To the guys of Tigereyes for providing a safe and supportive place. Thanks for your listening and acceptance.

To Julianne Santini for her helpful suggestions. Thank you for giving this your time and loving consideration.

To John Angelo and Karen O'Leary for their editing suggestions. Thank you for being so thoughtful and straightforward.

To Randy Benthien for his useful suggestions. Thanks for your on-going friendship and positive energy.

And to Bonnie Latham Lyon, my wife, best friend and life partner. You radiate the light of love so clearly. Thank you for choosing to travel with me and for all your support of this process. This work is dedicated to you.

PREFACE: HOW THIS BOOK GOT STARTED

The source of this book came into my awareness in 1994, at a time of great emotional pain. My marriage was disintegrating, a reality that I neither wanted nor felt I could accept. A portal, to deep and previously encased pain within my being, opened. I wrestled with this pain constantly. I found it overwhelming.

In March of 1994, I was grieving deeply on the floor of an upstairs room in my house when I realized that I couldn't do this anymore. I didn't know what to do and I believed that the pain would destroy me. I couldn't see beyond my grief. For the first time in my life I cried out for help, to whom I did not know. Like an abandoned and frightened child, between sobs I cried, "Help me! Help me! I can't do this anymore!" Then I lost consciousness for what seemed a short time.

When I became aware again, the silent word "write" was in my head. I got off the floor, grabbed a pen and began to write in a notebook. The sentences came without effort and I felt calm as I transcribed them. This is what I wrote.

> "The pain isn't the point. It always passes. And when it does, I am what remains. At the end, there is peace and silence. While there is pain, you doubt that the peace and silence exist. But they do.

The only way is through the pain. There are no easy ways. If easy ways existed, the whole world would be at peace. Resisting the pain creates war. So have your pain. Sob and sob on the floor, night after night, and you will see that it will ease. This pain is not for anyone else but you. Your pain. Stop making others responsible for it. You have it inside and it wants release and acknowledgement. It is the equilibrator and will restore inner balance.

After the storm of pain begins to subside, the dawn will begin to rise and you can let go of it all. Peace will come. What you will be then is what you have always been but never realized. What you knew as you, you will then know as false and not you. You will have shed it easily. There will be no need to hurt yourself or others. There will be no need for divisions but only acceptance and ease and love.

Then you will know that this happening now was all necessary because of where you were and where you needed to come. You will then know that you resisted this process very much but also knew that you could not remain where you were. This process takes time. Your time is ripening but there is more pain and more resistance to the pain yet to come. But you will stay with the sobs and anger and see them through and the pain will ease. You will wake up and find yourself anew. You will look back and bless the struggle.

It is all as it is to be. Have faith each day. Ask for help and I will assist and guide you. It will be given and you will make the journey. But ask, as you did tonight, and it will become easier. I help all who ask. Your struggle has a purpose. Your pain is your guide and friend and where you must be. Peace will appear.

This is the way it has always been throughout the ages. I have seen. It has always progressed in this way. I will not fail you as I have never failed others willing to ask for help, seek their truth and acknowledge their pain."

For the next ten years, writings like this came to me and I transcribed them. They usually came into my awareness after I had written in a journal about my thoughts, feelings and life circumstances. Discharging all my usual mental contents onto the pages of a journal seemed to open a mental space for the writings to enter my awareness. The ordinary journal entries were about the drama of my life. The transcribed writings were from a place beyond my personal drama but they counseled and comforted me and addressed specifics of my personal circumstances.

For a long time, I believed that the source of these writings was outside of me. I called that source, Father. I didn't know if Father was an angel, spirit guide, universal mind or other disembodied entity of some sort. I only knew that these words that came to me were wise and loving and helped me a great deal. I very much felt like a child learning from Father.

The initial writing was right. My pain did ease. I divorced. I experienced a three year period of grief with steadily declining intensity. I realized that this grieving process was only partially about my marital circumstances. It was a process of discovering an enormous amount of pain within, much older than my marriage. I learned that I could tolerate the pain and that it would pass. I learned that it wasn't necessary to completely understand the cause of the pain. Simply being present with the pain and allowing myself to experience it deeply appeared to be the key elements that led to release of the pain.

In 2004, the character of these writings changed. They became more generic, addressed no longer just to me but to all human beings. They are about the human experience of spiritual transformation. This book you hold is composed of the writings since 2004.

A fundamental concept in this book is that spiritual transformation occurs through detaching self-identity from the ego. This requires sufficiently expanded self-awareness to see the ego for what it is. In this book, this process is termed "ego dis-identification." Since the word ego means different things to different people, I would like to offer my understanding of the concept of ego as it is used in this book.

Ego can be seen as the self identity we have been conditioned to accept as who we are. It contains our personal history, physical body, beliefs, thoughts and emotional reactions. Ego sees itself as individual and separate from others. Initially, ego is invisible because we are so completely identified with it that we know no other self experience. Thus, it isn't "seen." The spiritual transformation allows us to know an expanded sense of self, referred to in this book as "Self", which holds and utilizes all the aspects of ego but does not identify with ego experience. The transformational movement away from ego identity leads to gradual atrophy of the ego experience. What remains is joy, the fundamental experience of being.

The transformational process does not occur as a result of reason but is due to shifts in awareness which expand the number and type of self experiences. At times you may find these writings confusing to your logical mind. This confusion may precipitate a shift in self experience useful for furthering the transformational process. So it is important to note your self experience, not only your thought reactions but also your sensations and emotions, as you read these words.

The book is composed of short writings, metaphors and stories. It doesn't matter if you read it in a linear, front-to-back manner or if you simply open it to any page and start reading. It is a book to be felt, sat with and read repetitively. Each word has its meaning and its energy to serve and assist you. Use it in a way that feels right for you, trusting your intuition.

I no longer feel that the source of these writings is outside of me. The book speaks of gaining assistance from "the disembodied ones" and perhaps that is part of the source. But it no longer feels separate from who I am. It is as if I was granted access to a wiser and expanded aspect of my consciousness. This place exists in you as well and perhaps you are already acquainted with it. It is the place where you and I and the disembodied ones are all one, without separation. This book is my Self talking with your Self in the place where we can both rest deeply in the experience of truth.

INTRODUCTION: FINDING YOUR SELF

One day you find yourself in this body, thinking these thoughts and surrounded by this physical world of plants, people and places. And when that day comes, you have accomplished a great deal because in order to find yourself here, you must have some sense that there are other realms of consciousness of which you have known or are a part. Otherwise there would be no finding at all. You would only know yourself as a body, having thoughts and experiencing this physical world with no sense of anything else.

For a long time we go around knowing ourselves as this type of person, with a certain personality type, coming from this family and having our personal goals and problems. I am the me that I tell myself I am in my mind of thought. This is the ego directed life. This is the life we have been taught to live by our elders and culture.

But this physical world experience has a way of showing us that we are more than what we have been taught. This physical world experience has a way of leading us to gray areas which bring into question the things we have been taught, gray areas that cause us confusion, uncertainty and growing unease. And if we are honest enough about our experience, if we are curious and courageous enough, we will want to know more. The old ways will begin to weaken and will not hold us as strongly.

But if we are not ready, are not honest, curious or courageous enough, we will find a way to discount that which is not consistent with what we have been taught so that the learned model remains intact and we find nothing other than this body, these thoughts and this physical world. We will find a way to avoid the gray areas and we will likely pay a great price for this. We may suffer greatly for this avoidance but we probably will not be aware of how we are avoiding or even the depths of our suffering.

But you and every other embodied soul are so much, much more than your thinking mind can imagine and the power you hold is enormous. The thinking mind has no idea, in fact cannot even conceive the idea, of the immense treasure that you are. You are a universe in which all possibilities exist and manifest. You are beyond time and separation. The experiences of time and separation do not exist within your true Self. What you are is beyond the ability of these words you are reading to communicate. What you are must be directly experienced to be known. And you are here to know the experience of your true Self because both you and this world you find yourself in so desperately need you to have this experience. The path to Self experience and the experiential knowing of Self are healing to not only this world of plants, people and places but on many other realms as well.

What you are reading is intended to support your journey to Selfhood. It is an attempt to identify common experiences along the way and to offer guidance and comfort. Your path of personal evolution is unique but you are accompanied by so many others on their paths and all of you will recognize many of the common experiences encountered.

THE PRODIGAL SON: A JOURNEY OF EGO DIS-IDENTIFICATION

We become lost to be found. The true homecoming cannot occur without first losing our way, without first seeing how life is with the ego in charge. There are some embodied souls who come into form already home. These few come only to serve. They have been here before and have already experienced the physical world drama to facilitate their spiritual transformations. They are no longer participants in the drama and come only to facilitate the spiritual transformations of other embodied souls. These beings do not become lost.

For the rest, it is necessary to become lost. Being lost is to be ego identified and to follow the enchantments of the senses and the cultural beliefs. It is also to be a prodigal son, to move away from our tribe and seek fulfillment in the world "out there". The prodigal son becomes dissatisfied with the tribal experience. He becomes restless and leaves the known of his earlier life experience. His hopes rise; he is filled with a sense of adventure and feels that great riches await him over the horizon. The prodigal son is largely, at least initially, driven by ego desires based on beliefs, mostly imprinted by the tribe. However, this adventuring is also what the soul desires, for the soul knows that the ego must weaken and surrender and that the journey of the prodigal son will produce this.

When the prodigal son sets out into the world an awakening is occurring. This takes the courage to leave the familiar behind and, often, to face much disapproval and criticism from the tribe. The journey's onset is often driven by restlessness and anger and the ego is both fearful and delighted at leaving the old behind. The ego feels that it is the tribe that is holding him or her back.

When the prodigal son leaves the tribal home, the ego is flexing its muscles and saying, "I am different than you. I know better. I am a unique and separate individual." Leaving the known tribal home is also a symbol of turning the attention inward and beginning to pay attention to internal experience. The mind is initially fascinated at the expansion in awareness of physical, mental and emotional experiences. The prodigal son finds initial delight in all of his/her various adventures, mostly involving the seeking of physical and emotional pleasure and attempts to aggrandize the ego. The prodigal son's awareness expands with each adventure and relationship, and, for a time, it is all wonderful and grand. When attention is directed inward, there is often a "honeymoon" period. The increased awareness of internal sensations and emotions may be experienced as pleasurable and a grand adventure.

Time passes and the "adventures" begin to seem familiar. The prodigal son witnesses himself doing many of the same things over and over. The adventures become increasingly stale and he begins to tire of himself. The riches over the horizon are never fully realized, even if material wealth is gained. The emptiness begins. He begins to hurt both emotionally and physically. As the awareness of the mental, emotional and physical experiences expands, previously unrealized pain surfaces and the initially pleasurable internal experiences give way to physical discomfort and distressing emotion. The ways of the ego no longer work and the body and psyche are shattering.

Time goes on and the prodigal son crashes into walls and falls down again and again. In attempt to relieve his suffering, the prodigal son seeks out more intense and varied experiences. Drugs, alcohol, sexual encounters and other intense sensory experiences may be sought to distract from the increasing physical and emotional pain. As the internally focused awareness experiences greater pain, the thoughts react and become alarmed and try to find solutions. The body wants to move and engage in different activities to relieve itself of the pain. The attention wanders and seeks other objects to attend to in order to escape awareness of the inner pain.

Eventually, he crashes and knows he cannot go on like this. He knows he does not know how to relieve his pain. He knows he needs to go home and ask for help. He knows he must surrender. None of the distractions have worked. The reality of the inner experiences can no longer be denied or escaped.

With the surrender to these realizations, his foundation of grief is released and he feels a new, more powerful and authentic layer of pain, one experienced with far fewer attempts at escape or distraction.

And yet, at the very same time, a new lightness begins to faintly glimmer, which allows him to better tolerate the foundational pain.

At this moment, he begins to realize that he is more than what he thought he was and, confused and disoriented, he begins his steps towards his father's house, which is also his house and home.

He arrives at the feet of his father, torn apart and defenseless, and surrenders his whole being into his father's open and joyous embrace. He is buoyed up by something much greater than himself and yet, it is what he is also.

This is when new energy can begin to flow from the father into the son and quicken the expansion of consciousness. The body has transitioned sufficiently to begin to accommodate the new energies. The ego has weakened enough to surrender and accept the greater embrace. Self identity has softened and become less defined and more expansive.

At this time on the Earth, many are finding emptiness in their worldly adventures, feeling battered and tired, and have begun the journey home.

Many are healing in the embrace of the father, losing their egos to become the greater selves they have always been.

And there are those who have healed and expanded and are partnering with the father to serve all those seeking home.

⟫⟩◈⟨⟪

THE PHYSIOLOGY OF
TRANSFORMATION

As the spiritual transformative process unfolds, energy is delivered through the top of the head (the crown chakra) and down into the spinal cord. With each unit of energy delivered, the spinal cord is being altered to accommodate the increased energetic load. The cord does not enlarge but its interior structure is being remodeled. It is like new cable being installed, replacing the old. The new cable has far greater capacity and conductivity. Although the spinal cord is being remodeled, it will assume the same size and occupy the same area of space in the body. Its conductivity and capacity, however, is being logrhythmically increased. This is an energetic and physical process that occurs in concert with expanding consciousness. It occurs only after there has been a great deal of prior physical transformative work initiated by the development of inner directed attention and awareness.

The physical transformative work, prior to the imparting of greater energies to the body through the crown chakra, is primarily musculoskeletal. Gross areas of tightness and limitation of movement are gradually released. With this release, the stored emotional experiences, held within the musculoskeletal system, are also released. Thus this process is a time for experiencing more intense physical sensations and emotions. Maintaining awareness of the physical sensations and emotions with an attitude of surrender is the way to most easily allow this transformation to do its work of bodily preparation for the greater energies. This process dissipates great energy and can be physically draining. If the ego-mind assumes control, it will find the process most unpleasant and frightening. It will call it illness and madness, and will attempt, in countless clever ways, to distract from and interrupt this transformative process. In fact, the ego knows that this process will result in its own death. This is the reason so many people experience death images during the transformation. Dreams of death, transformation and birth are common and are the imagistic representation of what is actually occurring in the body and psyche.

Much of the musculoskeletal release occurs along the spine. This ultimately eliminates any significant compressions on the neural structures that have been impeding neural impulses and energy conduction.

The muscular release allows for more efficient breathing and integration of prana or life force. The muscular release affects more and more subtle layers of physical tension in the body, thus, reducing the possibility of the return of compression on the neural structures (spinal cord, nerve roots and countless finer nerves in the spinal area). The nervous system is a major conduit of life force and energy. Part of increasing its capacity is the removal of these musculoskeletal obstructions.

The muscular release also facilitates the first phase of emotional release or grieving. Unreleased emotional experience is held in soft tissues, resulting in muscular tension and limitation of movement. As one grieves and releases emotion, muscular tension is lessened and movement becomes more fluid. Conversely, as muscles are eased through physical therapy, massage or other forms of bodywork, emotions are often mobilized and directly experienced.

When this physical transformation has progressed sufficiently, the new energies begin to enter the body and this is accompanied by the expansion of consciousness. At this point, there is usually more mus-culoskeletal release work to be done and more emotions to be released. However, it is at this time that the neurological changes begin to ac-celerate in the spinal cord. Many glandular changes also occur, includ-ing activation of the pineal gland and enlargement of the thymus. The activation of the pineal gland is necessary for the development of su-praordinary consciousness beyond the physical senses. Expansion of the thymus is needed to allow greater energy conductivity through the non-neurological energy channels throughout the body. When this oc-curs, the embodied soul experiences finer vibrational bodily sensations and much enhanced physical energy and endurance.

SURRENDERING INTO UNKNOWING TO FIND KNOWLEDGE

Surrender. Surrendering is called for all along the path. Each surrender is a letting go of another aspect of what you believed yourself to be. Each surrender asks you to come into unknowing. Each surrender releases more emotional tension from the body and increases the life force of your being. With each surrender, you allow in more help because you are admitting that you do not know, and this allows those who are able to serve you to now come to you.

When the prodigal son sets out on his own, away from the tribe, he is surrendering to the restless ego and also, deeply unconsciously, to the soul, for the soul knows this journey must happen. He is so full of his own knowing. He knows how grand the world is and how wonderful and talented he is and what he shall experience and gain.

Throughout his journey, the prodigal son meets with disappointments and small victories. As the disappointments mount and the victories become less victorious, there is a series of partial surrenders to reality. However, the ego is largely able to rationalize these away for quite some time. It is only when either the series of adventures loses all charm and begins to seem wearisome, or when a great trauma occurs, such as an illness, a painful ending of a relationship, a death or great failure, that the next major surrender occurs. This is the surrender to the truth of one's pain and fallibility.

The ego may re-group and again seek fulfillment out in the world. But ultimately, nothing changes and his pain only becomes greater and harder to deny.

When the prodigal son reaches the point where he knows he does not know and knows he needs help, it is the ego that is beginning its surrender into death. This is absolutely necessary for the life of light and truth to be realized.

Like a person who has just been told that they have a terminal illness, the prodigal son feels great pain at the realization of its limitations and the truth of its self deception and harm done to others. There may also be great loneliness now felt as he begins to experience his great distance from the father. There may be great regret over the enormous time lost in neglect of the need for the father. So, in this surrender, the son surrenders to a deeper truth of pain and to the fears of the ego death.

But the greatest surrender comes in the embrace of the father. This is the final dissolution of all that the son believed himself to be. It is the final descent into full unknowing and merging with the presence of the father. This is the final death of the ego, eliciting the greatest fear, that leads to the realization of unlimited joy, the joy which comes from the complete realization of Self as manifestation of the father. Through complete surrender, he comes to know that he is the father and is the joy and radiance of the father everlasting.

He experiences complete surrender into unknowing to find the most complete knowledge of the father.

THE LIGHT OF UNITY

Ultimately there is only light and this light is the father and the son and all that is, manifest and unmanifest. Everything seen with the physical eyes emits a light, which the physical eyes cannot see. It is only with the development of the pineal gland and corresponding supraordinary consciousness that this light, radiating from all things physical, may be seen. This light is a matrix upon which the physical object manifests. At a certain level of supraordinary consciousness, the physical manifestation, be it a living body or "inanimate" object, is no longer perceived. At this level of consciousness, the physical, as the senses know it, does not exist and all that is perceived is the light, which is unlike any physically perceived light. This light is the field and source of all that is manifest at the physical level. To perceive it while still in a human form is not uncommon. This light has been described many times throughout the history of humankind. This light is the most brilliant. The light of a billion stars pales in comparison. But unlike physically perceived light, it does not cause pain or distress to the physical structure. For to perceive the light is to have begun merging into the light and to have experientially realized the truth of one's essence, that one is not other than the father and the-all-that-there-is.

In this experience of merging with the light (or Self realization), the great eternal peace of timelessness is known. One enters the eternal moment of truth. This timeless now is represented by the chanting of

"Ohm" or "Amen" or "Aum." Many prayers end in "Amen", as if to say, "We who are in the physical field and conditioned to be limited by form, thought and word, sense in the core of our being that we are a part of the great oneness and that into this we shall eventually return, through an evolution of consciousness that will allow us to experientially know this truth, which we now only vaguely intuit."

Those who have known this light, find they cannot describe the experience, for no words can convey it. They know they have been given a glimpse of a deeper reality and they know this truth in the cells of their tissues. This experience may result in a lasting peace and, paradoxically, may be the catalyst for a restless seeking, born of a lack of fulfillment from that which previously satisfied.

These accelerated times of physical transformation and consciousness expansion will result in humankind living consciously in this light while still in form. Previously, this glimpse of the light of the-all-that-there-is was felt to be a special divine grace. It is now intended for all of humankind. It is both a catalyst for and the result of consciousness expansion.

———◆◇◆———

FEAR OF THE DISCIPLES

In the center of the chest is the heart chakra; the energy center in the body for the reception and transmission of love. Love is an enormous power and energy. In the presence of love energy, transformation occurs. The love energy dissolves all lower frequency energies and does so by bringing them up to its own frequency. Things of a lower frequency than love fear love, for they see love as their enemy and executioner.

This is the story of Jesus. Because he was unconditional love energy in human form, his energy was vastly greater than that of those around him. Even his disciples feared and doubted. They feared moving away from the tribe and they feared criticism and scorn. They feared their own transformative processes catalyzed by Jesus' love energy. They feared the death of their own egos. In these fears, they were no different than those who persecuted and crucified Jesus the Christ. The disciples however, unlike the persecutors, were unable to deny the truth of love's reality and power. Just as it is now, at the time of Jesus most of humankind were in denial of love and lived in fear and for survival. The disciples tasted Jesus' love and knew its truth and could not deny. This taste of the love energy and experience of the light was the catalyst for their journeys of spiritual evolution. Subsequently, the disciples spiritual journeys have, little by little, helped to catalyze the spiritual evolution of all of humankind over the last 2000 years.

When the love energy is experienced, the ego with its fearful reactive mind is transcended and dissipates, for it cannot co-exist within loves' radiance.

The river flows into the sea. The rivers' waters journey through many turns and turbulences, ever nearing the sea. And the day comes when the water reaches the rivers' end and pours into the vast sea, becoming one with the sea. It has lost its smaller identity and expanded into the oneness of the sea.

The passage from intellect and ego into love is what is happening at this time. In the body, it is the movement of energy and the structural transformation which allow for opening of the heart chakra and communication between it and the lower chakras.

This process requires ultimately only two things; surrender and awareness. The rest is beyond the abilities of any individual human. The rest is given. As a human becomes aware of the opening of the heart chakra and the expansion of its love energies, many things are brought into the individual awareness through the higher chakras, and, in a sense, they are passively received.

⎯⎯⎯◈⎯⎯⎯

FIRE

Surrender everything for love.

Watching the fire burn, you add a log from time to time. The flames are so beautiful and enchanting, calming you with their crackling and popping. Moving closer and adding another log, the heat increasing. Then fear arises and a warning thought of burning yourself. So you keep a safe distance, just enough to be warmed and enchanted but not burned. But after a while, it is not enough.

You want more, hotter, closer. And when the logs run out, you begin to put your belongings into the fire, one by one. First, the easy sacrifices. The old papers and magazines you no longer want, the lamp you never use and some old furniture covered with dust and spider webs from down in the basement. All useless stuff and now you wonder why you were hanging on to it all. As the fire is stoked you are drawn closer, warmed and vigilant to maintain the flames.

And now it becomes all you think about and you begin to fear that the fire will die out and leave you cold. So more things are put into it, now things harder to part with. The clothes you wore yesterday, the curtains, the dresser and the blankets. All consumed by the fire, giving radiance and heat.

Finally there is nothing left, just you and the fire. There is nothing else to feed it and the pain at the thought of being apart from it is now unbearable. The fire asks you to come into it and merge with it. You feel the final horror of the fear of death on one hand, and the fear of being without the fire on the other. Everything left of your ego tells you not to, as something deeper knows you will.

Like taking the first breath under water, you step into the flames and for a brief moment, the final death of the ego is a torment.

And then you know you have continued, somehow, and are aware. The fear is gone. Only light and bliss. Amen has come.

———⟫◆⟪———

LONELINESS

Fear not, for I am with you always. This is true, for I am. Remember this over and over because it is easy to forget until you are able to see the unseen.

On this journey, loneliness can be a great challenge. Your mind, conditioned by the tribe, has come to believe that you require approval and company. The ego desires to be seen, praised and recognized. The physical body longs for touch and tends to harden and immobilize without physical contact. As you lose the tribal conditioning of the mind, you begin to transform. There is a time when your transformation makes you a stranger in the world.

The tribe no longer seems relevant as you recognize its fear-based ignorance. And yet the ego still desires recognition and the body desires touch. But you have not yet developed great ability to see and know the unseen (for if you had, you would know, without any thought, that I am with you always). During this time, the loneliness can seem unbearable. You crave the contact and recognition and yet find yourself a stranger in a strange land where no contact or recognition even seems possible. This time is for the development of faith, a time to repeat over and over, "Fear not, for I am with you always." Your body may feel immediate comfort with the remembrance of these words, as if it were being caressed. In fact, it is being caressed, not by physical touch, but by energies and beings unseen, pouring their love, support and approval into you.

These words will bridge you from loneliness to the place where loneliness is no longer, for you will see and know and be one with those unseen others who have been loving you so.

It is during this time of loneliness, that many have forestalled their journeys through addictions. This often takes the form of plunging back into the world of the tribe with its offerings of intoxicants and stimulation of sensory diversions and sexual escapades, mostly devoid of true communion. Many have committed suicide, ending their bodily life in attempt to end the suffering of loneliness, to find themselves stalled on the same path, only now without their most recent physical form.

Eventually, to arrive home, all must successfully walk the bridge of faith over the dark chasm of loneliness to reunite with the countless others who have loved and supported them all along. Here true vision has been restored. Sight has returned to the blind.

After this point, there are many further challenges but the loneliness of the body/ego is no longer one of them.

⋘◆⋙

LEAVING BEHIND THAT WHICH IS NOT SELF

Abandon the old ways. Every step along this path asks you to leave something behind, so that it may seem that there is less and less of you going on with each step. With each step, you are in a new place and have abandoned the place in which the previous step placed you. The parts of you attached to the place you are in must be abandoned with the next step. And with the subsequent step, those aspects attached to this newer place must also be left behind. So it is a series of letting goes and leaving behinds, which leaves bits of you dropped beside each footprint.

The bits are the remnants of what you thought you were but now have realized are not. Alongside the bits in many places, the path is moist with tears. Tears shed from the pain of letting go and from the shock to the consciousness of the enormity of its ignorance in realization that the bit left behind was not your true Self but only a layer, tacked on by the tribe, which had restricted and hidden the true one for so long.

So, with each step, a new place is entered, a false bit is left behind, tears are shed and the true one emerges a bit more. To the old one they are bits of death, loss, grief and suffering with each step. To the true one, it is a birth, a contraction with each step, moving it closer to emerging fully into the light with joy, love and enormous power.

The path is the dynamic evolution of both the birth and the death simultaneously. The ego-mind often cannot hold it, so it is either in fear, and therefore resistance, or in confusion. Confusion is more useful because it can allow for the progression of the two unfoldings of birth and death, which are in essence only one.

This path can seem so lonely, as if absolutely no one is there with you. And, in fact, this path cannot unfold without continued effort, vigilance and intent on the part of the journeying one.

However, it is more like a race, wherein one is running with many others, each providing the effort and energy for their own steps forward. But to see the others along with you inspires many steps forward. And along the sidelines there are countless others, cheering and applauding you on. Initially, these others on the sidelines may not be seen but a certain distance along the path, their presence, encouragement and energetic support begin to be perceived and inspire the journeying one greatly.

But this is not a race with a finish line and a winner. It is a way which seems a path of grief and loneliness, becoming an inspired and supported journey and, ultimately, becomes a merging with the divine true one and the dynamic evolution of constant creative manifestation everlasting as God-love expresses itself evermore in never-ending forms.

———◈———

LENGTHENING: BALANCING THE UPWARD AND DOWNWARD FORCES

As the process of spiritual evolution unfolds, an upward pull is often felt. In the body, it is an upward force exerted upon the skull and axial skeleton. The disc spaces between the vertebral bodies are widened and nerve roots exiting the spinal cord are decompressed. The release of downward muscular tension and painful emotion discussed before are a part of this process, but the upward force upon the body is a related but separate phenomenon.

The life of humankind on this planet is dominated by gravity. This constant downward force literally pulls the body down into the Earth. It is also the physical counterpart of the non-physical downward energy which roots one to this Earth home. Without the Earth-rooted energies grounding one, there is a tendency to become cognitively oriented and to lose contact with emotions and somatic sensations. Gravity is a physical force upon the body; the Earth-rooted energies are not, but are an essential element to be opened to and appreciated, in order to fully evolve spiritually while still in human form.

In addition to the physical downward pull of gravity, the emotion-al/physiologic response patterns generated by the ego-mind produce significant downward force upon the body. The ego reactions of fear, resistance and anger usually occur with a "hunkering down" physiology. The muscles tighten, the axial skeleton compresses and contracts downward and forward and the physiology shifts in a way which generally dampens the flow of healing and pro-life energies within the body and psyche.

The physiology of the ego driven personality combined with gravity have resulted in the premature end of many physical lives and the near halting of the spiritual evolutionary process.

The counterforce to the Earth-rooted energies is the energy which produces the upward pull upon the body. There are many non-physical entities related to and supportive of each human embodied soul. Each human is in constant energetic connection with many of these non-physical entities, which may be said to be their "spiritual family." When the human is ego dominated and pulled densely down into the earth, the energetic connection with its "spiritual family" is weak and the non-physical entities are limited in the amount of energy and support they can give because the receiving capacity of the human being has become poor.

However, when sufficient surrender has occurred and the physical/emotional release transformation has progressed to a certain point (and this is to say, a significant amount of grieving has occurred), the obstructions to reception of the upward energies from the non-physical ones have lessened and greater assistance may be given and received. These upward energies facilitate the bodily healing and transmission of life force through the physical structure and psyche. This additional energy facilitates the entire spiritual evolution.

Receiving the energies from the non-physical "spiritual family" is essential in optimally opening the heart charka and transitioning the embodied one away from the ego driven life to the life directed by light and love.

There are some who are dominated by the upward energies and have little counterbalancing from the downward energies of Earthrootedness. These are soul consciousness identified beings that have great difficulty managing their physical lives and bodies. It is difficult for them, at times, to recall that they are embodied. They often neglect the physical nurturing of the body. Their sleep is erratic. They eat unevenly and with little joy. They are often prone to accidents and injuries and have few routines. They are prone to illness and depression and have little somatic awareness.

These souls require greater awareness and development of their Earth-rooted energies. They must recall that they are in human form, which is of the Earth. And like the Earth, these bodies exist in the rhythms of night and day and seasonal change. They need to recall that the body is built to live in rhythms; rhythms of sleep and wakefulness, rest and action, thought and feeling, social contact and solitude, stimulation and quiet, and laughter and tears. The greater the development of the Earth-rooted energies, the more comes the realization that the body is a miraculous instrument to be played by the soul in service on Earth. The Earth-rooted energies help to develop respect and gratitude for the body and its Earthly rhythms, without increasing the soul's identification with the body. Only the ego-mind and the gravitational pull deceive the soul into body identification and seeing the physical world as the only reality.

Most of humankind is overly identified with the body and overly invested in the physical experience. Therefore, most have, as their spiritual tasks, the development of the upward energies and concomitant physical, emotional and energetic transformative processes. For those dominated by the upward energies, the task is development of bodily awareness and respect, and of living in harmony with the Earth rhythms.

The embodied ones on the Earth have come to use their bodies to perform specific functions in the physical plane. When the upward energies from the spiritual family are balanced with the earth rooted energies, the physical life becomes soul, not ego, directed and the physical life is lived in the light and radiance of love.

FEAR IN THE UPPER ABDOMEN

It may seem a paradox that in order to evolve into the soul directed life, which has transcended the ego and dis-identified with the body, much attention to and awareness of the bodily experience usually must occur.

Conscious attention to the somatic process is a great stimulant to the physical and energetic transformations. Awareness of this process without judgment is the key. Awareness of sensations with judgments about what it means or if it is a "good" or "bad" experience, indicates that the ego-mind is present and resisting. In this case, attention to the somatic experience will not facilitate the transformation. What usually is occurring is a recycling of ego-based cognitions and emotions about the somatic experience, which impedes the forward movement of the transformation.

A core transition point in the body is in the upper abdomen and diaphragm. A huge amount of ego resistance is usually encountered at this physical site. It is mostly in the experience of fear. Energetically, this is the point where movement naturally tends to extend upward and, thereby, enter and assist in opening the heart chakra. This movement from the third to fourth chakra is correlated with significant dis-identification from the ego and the beginning of living in love's light. This is the difficult point of merging with the fire. So the ego, sensing its death is close at hand, mounts its greatest resistance. This is usually experienced as constriction in the diaphragm and solar plexus, and as fear, which frequently manifests indirectly as anger.

Each human has usually lived many years directed by the ego-mind, with its emotional/physiologic responses over and over driving the physical structure deeper into the gravitational pull. At the solar plexus, the torque of the downward and forward bending forces is at its greatest and, as a result, the constriction of the upper abdomen and diaphragm has become an armored layer, like a thick walled castle built to protect its ego-king.

Thus, the amount of physical/emotional transformative work required in this area is usually quite large. As this work is being done, the capacity to receive the assistance from one's spiritual family gradually increases. This, in turn, further facilitates the physical/emotional release process.

As this occurs, the physical body to some degree literally extends upward and outward, around the fulcrum of the solar plexus. The energies entering the heart chakra increase from both below and above. The experience of love occurs more frequently and profoundly as the transformation progresses.

———◆———

THOUGHT: EGO'S ATTACHMENT
POINT TO THE SELF

Through these transformative processes, one moves towards dis-identification from and yet a profound respect for the body. It is seen as a beautiful instrument to be utilized respectfully in the service of the love energy and higher consciousness directed life. It is a movement from "I am my body" to "What an amazing body tool I have been given."

So it is with the relationship between the cognitive mind and consciousness. Initially the ego consciousness identifies itself with, not only its bodily form, but also its thinking. "I think, therefore, I am" becomes the mantra of the cognition identified self. As the transformative processes unfold, consciousness gradually dis-identifies with thought. Consciousness begins to be aware that thought is generally ego-based and is only a small subset of the totality of its awareness. Consciousness begins to see that thought is unceasing and reactive. As consciousness begins to see thought as separate from the true Self, the ability of thinking to cause physiologic reactions lessens and the body becomes calmer, even when the thoughts are reactive and judgmental. Consciousness begins to see that very little of thought content is useful or reality based. There are times when thought is useful; the learning of new and constructive cognitive skills and information, as the primary tool for verbal and written communication with other formed beings and in certain situations of analytic problem solving. In these instances, consciousness knows thought to be a useful tool and gift to be used appropriately. But it is also noted with unmistakable clarity how thought is mostly ego derived and defensive in nature. The ego derived thought serves solely to protect the ego's existence and, therefore, has no usefulness to the higher consciousness. As ego's main mode of protection, thought content is seldom reality based or oriented in the present. Almost all thoughts are about the past or future. Many are about judgments or assumptions and, therefore, incongruent with the experienced truth of the present moment. By merely attaching itself to thought, consciousness has been tricked out of the present moment. For when consciousness is truly anchored in the present there is primarily the experience of non-cognitive awareness and this experience is known as sufficient unto itself without the need for thought. This is what higher consciousness truly is, full awareness of this moment, without time and wanting nothing. Consciousness knows that thought takes it away from this experience and moves it towards ignorance and anxiety.

Therefore, the higher Self comes to see cognition as a useful tool in some circumstances (and far less useful an instrument than is the body) but mostly as an ignorant habit requiring vigilance and discipline to break. Thinking is the greatest addiction, indeed, the sole life blood, of the ego. Without thought, the ego cannot exist and cannot direct the life of the human.

As the transformative path continues, consciousness sees this so clearly and also comes to know the great challenge in dis-identifying from ego-based thought.

As the path continues and ego-based thought has diminishing influence upon the Self, a whole new experience of thought emerges.

⋙◆⋘

EMERGENCE OF THOUGHT
BEYOND EGO

Initially, consciousness is one with the body and thought. As a result of the transformative processes, consciousness begins to witness the somatic sensations and ego-based thinking. The expanding consciousness sees the body as a useful instrument with which it may engage in the world of physicality. The body is now known to be an antenna, capable of receiving energy and knowledge from non-physical realms. Somatic sensations become the "language" of the physical body and the embodied soul becomes able to understand this physical language. Consciousness comes to know the difference between useful and not useful, truth and not-truth, and that which supplies vitality and that which is toxic by means of the somatic sensations. In essence, the body feels whether a substance is healthy or toxic, whether a person speaking is representing truth or not-truth or whether a situation or experience is useful or not useful and the consciousness becomes capable of interpreting these somatic feelings. Thereby, the body, although not seen as Self by consciousness, becomes recognized as a useful allay and vehicle.

As stated before, at the level of mental experience, consciousness comes to recognize most thought as ego-based and potentially inhibitive of truth realization. When consciousness gains a certain level of dis-identification from ego-based thought, the recognition of non-egoic thought may be developed. Ego-based thought has associated unhealthy reactive patterns of physiologic change. These may be experienced as the emotions of distress or excitement with the accompanying stimulated physiology. When non-egoic thought is experienced, the body feels calm and the soul is at peace. The experience is soothing and nurturing, and consciousness recognizes that it is receiving knowledge and guidance from the non-physical realms. This silent verbal guidance is received through the higher (above heart chakra) energy centers in the body and is associated with the upward energies. The upward energies are a plethora of energies like a cable carrying countless channels, each with unique aspects and benefits to the unfolding embodied soul. One of these energies is the "channel" of non-egoic thought. It is a "direct line" to guidance and truth, which is instantly recognized as such by the somatic sensations and the associated quietude. When this experience is initially encountered, the ego rises up with thoughts of resistance. The embodied soul may doubt the truth of the non-egoic thoughts for a time and the doubt is entirely due to ego-based thought, for, once again, the ego is in fear and must assume its defense in the face of this threatening truth development. However, consciousness usually comes to acceptance of the truth of the non-physical guidance, for it recognizes the peace and calm of the experience and this eventually overrides the chatter of the fearful ego. The embodied soul comes to place great trust in the messages received in this way. This guidance from the upward energies allows the embodied soul to successfully encounter the resistance of the ego and lack of support from the tribal environment and culture.

THE DIRECT EXPERIENCE OF LOVE

Until you have the direct experience of love, you do not know how profoundly you are loved. You are continually bathing in love-light. It surrounds you always. The direct experience of love cannot be mistaken for anything else. The love experience instantly dissolves any other energies in your being, which are lower than the frequency of love. In this instant, all non-love aspects of self experience are no longer known. The sense of being an individual self is lost. Continual joy, wonderment and gratitude are found. This love union is not of the temporal world and is of the ongoing present and, therefore, cannot be measured in minutes or hours. The consciousness merged with love no longer thinks in terms of units or labels because all has become one. With this union, consciousness realizes all has always and forever been one and that she has never been separate from love.

Ego can only function in terms of division and separation and does not survive during consciousness' merger with the love energies. Ego is a lesser frequency energy of mental conditioning operating primarily by thought. Thought is not present in the experience of love. Love is the truth of the-all-that-there-is. Ego and thought are not fundamental reality. Ego and thought are constructions and aberrations. Because their frequencies cannot co-exist with love energy, they can never directly experience love. They, therefore, do not know it or believe in it. As noted earlier, they only sense its danger to them and cannot help but function in such a way as to keep consciousness from the direct experience of love and to produce doubt in consciousness following a love merger experience. In this way, ego and its thinking patterns can be seen as anti-truth and anti-reality. The ego does not want you to know how loved you are. Because with the love experience and the deep knowledge of being love and being loved, consciousness develops great power in being, and any fear based needs for identification with the ego and its thought are much more easily dissolved.

The love experience may occur in many ways. The love experience may spontaneously envelop consciousness. It may be intuited without full consciousness by being in the presence of great beauty or a being of advanced spiritual evolution. It may be experienced after great suffering and a despairing cry for help or by one who, through belief and faith, has practiced vigilance over her intentions and behaviors, striving to be more loving and of more service to those around her.

However experienced, love once experienced can never be lost or fully forgotten. The love experience opens or widens the portals through which love's support enters. The conscious knowledge of being love, and being loved and supported, is expanded. The spiritual transformative processes are quickened, thereby. The AMEN has been experienced and the consciousness moves its "identity" more rapidly towards the loving AMEN.

⇒•◊•⇐

TRUTH WANTS IN: THE WOODS BOY

Along the path of spiritual unfoldment, many difficult experiences are encountered. The ego dies a slow death and rallies to mount defensive resistance in countless ways to divert from the direct experience of a difficult truth. To the senses, the physical world and tribal culture seem to support the reasoning and ways of the ego. And so, one can feel so alone on the journey home, alone until the support of the spiritual family is felt and realized as truth.

***

A woman married and gave birth to several children. She did her best to keep her house, and to teach and care for her children. And, for a time, all seemed to be going well.

One day she found the door to her house was cracked, apparently from being kicked. This disturbed her deeply but she kept silent about her inner discord and had the door replaced.

Sometime later, a window was found broken with a stone resting on the living room floor. She threw the stone back outside and replaced the window but her inner gnawing intensified.

Shortly after the window had been replaced, she and her children began to notice a disheveled child, standing at the periphery of the woods that encircled their home. At first the child pulled back deeper into the woods when he saw the others looking at him. Gradually, he became bolder and let them stare. Over time, he came closer and, eventually, knocked on the door. The woman's unease was intense and her children became frightened. They did not respond to his knocking.

As the days passed, the woods boy knocked more frequently and longer. He began to cry out to be let in. More windows were broken.

Although the woman's distress became great, she felt there was something familiar about this unruly child and she was oddly drawn to him. And then, with great shock, she knew who he was.

She walked to the door and opened it. Her children were afraid. The woods boy came in and she really saw him for the first time. She saw he was angry but mostly saw how tired, sad and afraid he was. He looked into her eyes; both his and hers filled with tears. This was the child she had birthed long ago and, because he and her circumstances at that time were not compatible, had given away. She had, without trying, buried those memories deep within her.

He had come back and could not be denied. He continued to look into her eyes, as if thirsty and drinking long from a cup.

"All I ever wanted was for you to see me," he said.

They both cried for a very long time.

The other children came into the room. They all embraced and he was never again shut out. The family changed and became whole. The woods boy was washed and fed. The family was stronger and at peace. The woods boy was now home. The family was now complete.

THE PRACTICE OF OPENING TO WHAT IS

The ego is not a malevolent enemy. Its presence obscures truth and the experience of joyful wholeness. Ego directed actions are most often harmful and result in suffering. But the ego itself is in pain and lives in fear, and identification with it results in suffering. As consciousness expands, ego is seen from a distance and is known as the product of tribal beliefs and conditioning. The collective consciousness of the tribe is limited and so ego has limited vision and knowledge. It sees the individual and knows separation; it does not know wholeness or connection. The ego is created from a lack of the experience of love and, because the final truth is love and wholeness in which the ego cannot sustain a separate identity, it is afraid and behaves to preserve and defend itself. The ego is derived from ignorance of truth. Although the ego acts in ways to further its separation and produce suffering (its own and others), ultimately it wants union with the father. It wants to be one with the family of the-all-that-there-is. Like the woods boy, it has been separated from the mother and like the prodigal son, he has been thrashing about in the world, thinking he wants accolades and adventures. The truth is that he longs for mother union but the fear of the transformative process, requiring the letting go of all he has known, keeps him from the realization of this longing.

Previously, it has been noted that the evolving consciousness increasingly sees ego as not-Self and knows it must maintain great and constant vigilance to avoid re-attachment to ego. Consciousness comes to realize that "doing battle" with the ego is futile. Forcefully resisting the ego increases suffering and blocks movement of the higher energies. What is called for is recognition of ego as not-Self and, at the same time, opening the door of the house of the heart chakra to ego, sending it love and feeling both its longing to and fear of entering. It must neither be shut out nor dragged in. Eventually, it will respond to keeping the door open and looking into its eyes with judgeless compassion. In many ways, it just wants to be seen; truly seen, in a way it cannot see itself. This is all that is required for the alchemy to occur.

The practice of sending love is powerful. Love can be sent to others or situations outside of yourself and can be sent to the places of resistance within you. Practice being the embracing father. Practice being the mother, overcoming her fear to open the door widely. This practice is powerful. You will find resistance melting in the forms of improved relationships, healing of disease and softening of the body, increasing peace and greater awareness of the present moment with a lessening of interest in the past or future.

This process of systematically opening to the moment's truth, surrendering to it and sending love to that which is in resistance is alien to the ego-mind. Many get stuck in resisting that which is in resistance. It is called "bad". The ego is present when the embodied soul identifies with being "one on the spiritual path." Anything encountered which is perceived to be an obstacle to spiritual progress is judged, resisted and attacked. Here the ego is still present and in control. This spiritual war results in little evolution of consciousness. The "spiritual ego" is also present when judgments are made about differing spiritual techniques or schools. The evolving consciousness comes to know that all teachings may lead to the essential truth of Oneness and so does not judge or resist any of them.

Regardless of the school or technique, the essence is awareness, recognition of resistance, surrender and sending love to that in resistance. This process does not require dogma or a name.

THE SPECIFIC FUNCTION OF THE EMBODIED SOUL

Many of you are being called at this time to perform special functions. Some of you are clearly aware of this, for you have received inner guidance resulting in certain knowledge about what it is you are being called to do. Many others are being called by the formless ones to take on certain tasks but are not aware that they are being called. Others have knowledge of what they are being called to do but are resisting performing those functions because of fear and doubt.

Know that you are here to perform a function. It may be the same function or a series of different functions to be performed throughout this physical lifetime. Whether you are to serve a single function or multiple functions, the result is to assist the evolution of human consciousness. At this time, the evolutionary movement has been intensified and all beings are needed to perform their tasks in order to bring humankind to greater consciousness.

You will know when you are performing your function for the benefit of all humankind. When you are doing what you are called to do, you feel great energy in the body. You are operating from love energy. The work itself is fulfilling and is not performed simply to attain a specific outcome. You feel energized and "right" in the performance of this work. The sense of time is often lost and attaining and maintaining attentional focus on the work seems natural and easy. The work becomes your primary concern and objective. You can be sure you are not performing "called to" work if it is experienced as enervating, overly effortful and unfulfilling. "Called to" work is renewing and often feels effortless. One feels great privilege in being able to perform this work.

For those who sense their task of purpose but are halted by fear or doubt, know this; there is an inviolable law of energy which guarantees not only your survival but your fulfillment and success when you take consistent action towards performing your function. When you engage in your "called to" work, energy channels are literally opened in you. The love energy flows more fully and enhances your power. You become more magnetic to other beings and your work is of excellence and affects others in profound ways. This results in provisions for you; provisions of relationships, work opportunities, finances and material needs. This law does not fail. It only appears to fail when one is not truly performing their "called to" function.

For those who do not experience being called to a particular function, it is best to perform the duties of each day already in your awareness without complaint or resistance. It is best to avoid trying to figure out your purpose. Accept where you are now in this lifetime. Pause to notice more and increase your awareness of your somatic sensations. The things you see, hear and feel will eventually lead you to the state of knowing what it is you are being called to do. This may not occur for a long time. Not all embodied souls are being called to serve particular functions at this time. Many of you are to learn through experience and expand awareness without performance of a specific function. When consciousness evolution has reached the correct level for the task, the embodied soul will be called and the process of knowing will begin. Even before the performance of your specific function, your process of consciousness expansion in preparation for your function will affect those you contact in a powerful way.

Some will live long in their bodies before ever being called and their specific function may be fulfilled in a very short time. Others perform their functions continuously throughout the entire physical life. The value of each of these functions is equal.

⟹•◇•⟸

EGO'S AMBIVALENCE

Know that nothing essential may ever be taken from you. The ego-mind is very concerned with acquiring and retaining things it considers essential to its wellbeing and survival. The ego functions from a place of lack because it has unconscious knowledge of its artificiality. Because ego unconsciously knows that it is not based in fundamental truth, it experiences inadequacy and shame, and attempts to fulfill itself by protecting its image, defending its material possessions and relationships and by attempting to acquire more and more "stuff" (material possessions, skills, attention, prestige and approval.) Because ego ceases to exist in the presence of love energy and because love energy is the fundamental truth, ego is illusory.

Ego, having an unconscious awareness of its tentative position in reality, is unstable and fearful. Ego operates, on one hand, to survive and by immersing in the physical and sensory world as its only reality and by attempting to gain ever increasing material wealth and status at that level of experience, it believes it shall survive. On the other hand, the ego unconsciously knows that it is not love, that love is the only true reality, and that it cannot survive. Ego unconsciously longs for relief from its delusional existence. Thus, ego also seeks to destroy itself. Like the moth to the flame, it ultimately cannot resist being drawn to the truth of love. Ego sometimes behaves in ways to cause early termination of the physical body. The ego identifies itself with the body it inhabits and erroneously concludes that if the body dies, it will also. And so ego is often driven to develop life shortening physical addictions, place itself in situations of physical danger or to intentionally kill the body through suicide.

Ego, however, is an error in consciousness and does not end with the end of the bodily life.

There are varying levels of ego consciousness. Slightly more evolved ego consciousness does not behave to prematurely end the life of the body, but rather continues the life of acquisitiveness until the natural conclusion of dissatisfaction and suffering. In this way, the ego begins its dissolution by psychic, emotional and spiritual pain without direct or intentional harm to the physical body. This weakening of ego allows for emergence of conscious knowledge that the ego ways are unfulfilling and the embodied soul often recognizes the need to ask for help. The prodigal son, at this point, represents the state of a weakened and partially surrendered ego with consciousness beginning to dis-identify from ego. He is confused and beginning to seek guidance from a truer source than ego-mind.

LESSONS OF THE PIERCED HEART

A common image, reproduced in many ways throughout the history of humankind, is the sword-pierced heart. This has been a part of religious art for thousands of years. The sword is seen penetrating the open and vulnerable heart, blood dripping from the exit wound and sword tip. This raw image may be experienced with tightening in the chest and constriction of the breath.

An arrow has often substituted for the sword. The arrow-pierced heart brings associations with Cupid, the agent of the tribal notion of love, which is not love at all but rather an emotionally intense period of projection onto another being that produces the transient and intoxicating illusion of self-completion. The chemicals produced in the physical body during this experience are highly addictive and many human beings stall their progress on the path by the pursuit of repeating this "love" experience as soon as it dissipates. The image of Cupid-love conjures up feelings of humor and longing.

So the pierced heart may represent both suffering and longing. And it is a violent image; a ripping open of the most sensitive and vulnerable organ in the body, naturally leading to the death of the body.

Human beings long to directly experience love, not the romantic tribal version, but immersion in the ultimate truth of ever new love light. The embodied soul is like the river's waters, rushing towards the ocean, longing to merge and be reunited.

Suffering is the necessary price to be paid for the gradual weakening and ultimate death of the ego. The heart must be opened so that unrealized truths may be directly experienced. This is painful and the ego-mind fears the pain. The pierced heart bleeds its truth and eventually there is no more blood to pump. The consciousness sees and experiences the fear-based ways of the ego until the trickery no longer deceives. The pierced and exsanguinated heart can no longer support the body and so physical death ensues. The seen and known ego can no longer captivate the identity of consciousness and so weakens and eventually dies. Freed from ego identification, consciousness is released into the experience of its truer nature. The longing for love ceases because consciousness experiences itself as love, merged and whole.

Without this transformative journey of bleeding the truth and exsanguinating the ego, the longing can never be sated. The thirst will be ever present until the waters of true love light pour forth and fill the soul.

One may smile and giggle at the Cupid heart for the soul sees the humor in the parody of love propagated by the tribal conditioning. In the eyes of love energy, Cupid's love is slapstick with elements of both comedy and tragedy.

In the images where the sword is vertical, it represents the spine and the vast energies available to the individual human. The sword is a symbol of great power and there is no greater power in the universe than that of love. In order for the love energies to vitalize and empower the human being, the heart chakra must be opened so that the love energy can flow through this portal, channeling through the spinal cord and nerves and up into the brainstem and brain, catalyzing the development of expanded consciousness and supraordinary awareness. This energy, resultant from the heart chakra opening, allows greater access and receptivity to the upward energies generated by the formless ones.

—⋙◆⋘—

FAITH

I wish to speak more about faith. You came from the love light that is the source of all things, manifest and unmanifest; and into it you shall return when you leave this present body. In fact, you have never left the light, the source of your being. It radiates from you and around you while you are in this form. Those with sufficiently evolved consciousness can see this light that you are, for they have developed vision beyond that of the usual capacity of the physical eyes.

This light is your truth. You have not separated from this powerful divine love. You remain that which the father is.

You have simply adopted a human form at this time. Your body and the physical life experience you are having are both extremely precious and meaningful and yet, they are a minute fraction of the totality of what you are.

The body, infused with the divine love light that is what you are, is capable of recognizing truth. The ego with its mind of thought is not. When the body is in the presence of truth, the love light brightens and flows with greater energy through the body. All human beings have the capacity to recognize or feel this energy activation. This recognition may be conscious or unconscious. If awareness is attending to the thoughts of the ego-mind, the expansion of energy in the body due to the presence of truth will go unrecognized consciously. If awareness is attending to the wordless sensations of the body, it will consciously recognize the shift in energy and, with sufficient experience, will come to equate these energy expansion sensations with truth recognition.

Faith is related to truth recognition. Even when truth recognition is mostly unconscious (usually because of ego-mind interference), it is subtly present in awareness. Faith is the willingness to speak or act in accordance with the subtle, largely unconscious, recognition of the truth. Faith takes a stand on this subtle recognition in the face of the disapproval and invalidation often found in the tribal environment. Faith results from the tiniest of glimmers of the felt truth that one, in fact, is divine light. Faith is what allows one to persevere in spite of the fearful antagonism of the ego-mind. The essential truth, that a human being is first and foremost the divine light of love, is what creates the ultimate failure of the ego.

Faith is a manifestation of the recognition of truth.

<hr>

THE REMEMBRANCE OF LOVE

Fear is resistance. Love accepts resistance. The natural consequence to the presence of love is the unraveling of fear. By practicing the remembrance of the presence of love (the light which pervades all things), your identification with the light increases and your direct experience of the love light grows.

Most people are taught to believe that difficulties and resistances are outside of themselves, in outer situations or others. Accompanying each one of these encounters of outer resistance is an inner resistance. A person experiences an outer difficulty, perhaps the unwanted behavior of another person, and mounts an inner experience of resistance. This may manifest as anger, fear, tightening of the breath and muscles, restricted movement, alterations of blood flow and neurological impulses, impedance of energy flow through the spinal cord, nerves and meridians, and changes in endocrine secretions.

When practicing the remembrance of love, the initial tendency may be to attempt to accept and send love to the other or outer situation. There is great benefit in so doing. However, the effectiveness of the remembrance of love is much more powerful when first applied to the inner resistance; to first be aware of, accept and send light to the inner resistance initiated by the situation or other.

Each time inner resistance is recognized, it can be accepted and surrendered to, and by remembering one's essence of love light, love energy can intensify and radiate to the emotional and physiologic man-ifestations of the resistance. The inner resistance is fear. The remem-brance of love can be sent to the aspect of ego in fear, like the woods child who just wants to be seen in the light of the mother's eyes.

Each time this is done, a little more of ego is able to merge with love's fire. The embodied soul begins to discover that fear and its physi-ologic expressions become a less frequent experience and, in its place, love's light brightens

As the practice of the remembrance of love is applied to the inner resistance, the human being notices that outer resistances are encoun-tered less frequently. This is a result of the growing intensity of love en-ergy in the person practicing the remembrance of love. When the other or situation in resistance experiences the presence of the greater love radiating human, the fear in the other or others is soothed and often the situation is shifted to one of non-resistance without any particular action required. Fear is leached out of the situation by the greater pres-ence of love radiating from the embodied soul practicing the remem-brance of love.

⟫◆⟪

BIRTH OF THE ILLUSION OF SEPARATION

The story of Adam and Eve is the story of the birth of ego. They ate from the tree of knowledge and saw that they were naked and were ashamed. The fruit from the tree of knowledge was the apple. Thinking began when it was eaten. The cognitive aspect of mind was born and began its quest for things and the need for experiences to have words and explanatory concepts. And so a buffer between the experience and the one having the experience developed. The cognitive mind of knowledge would not be at ease unless the thing or experience had a name. Further, the cognitive mind needed to understand the relationships between objects, beings and experiences. It sought explanations for why things were the way they were and could not rest or accept until it believed it understood the whys and hows of its experiences.

With the eating of the apple, Adam and Eve saw with new eyes. These new eyes saw only the physical manifestations of the-all-that-there-is and saw that things were separate and different from one another. Adam and Eve saw that they were in bodies of flesh and bone and that their bodies had anatomic differences. They felt alone, isolated and unsafe. As a result, they felt shame; the sense that the self they were seeing with these new eyes of knowledge was not enough and was not whole.

From that perspective they were correct.

Before knowledge, they experienced their connection with Oneness and found joy in the never-ending variation of the manifestations of Oneness; a great wonderful kaleidoscope of creation, with each manifestation being unlike any other and yet all knowing their union with the other manifestations of the Oneness.

After the apple, they lost their knowing but gained specific limited vision and a questioning, categorizing and quantifying mind. They then, for the first time, felt the desire to cover themselves so the specific vision of the other could not see their differences or inadequacies.

So with the knowledge of the apple came limited knowing and a perceived loss of wholeness and the restless search for fulfillment.

⇒◆⇐

WOLF BOY

It is time to come into all of your power. At this time, your power is dearly needed. The earth needs healing. The ways of humankind need healing. The healing occurs as each of you comes into your full power. You are invited and encouraged to become the God you truly are.

Like the boy who was raised by wolves, who thought he was a wolf and knew the ways of wolves and behaved like a wolf, you are far more than what you have been taught to believe you are. What you have been taught to see as yourself and how to behave and what to believe as truth has come from a place of very limited consciousness.

How strange an experience it was for the wolf boy when he found himself, away from the pack and in the presence of humans. He sensed his kinship with them. He was excited and fearful and told himself, "No, you are only a wolf. Don't be ridiculous." A sweet painful conflict he felt as he gazed upon his brethren who seemed to him so powerful and miraculous and spoke in such a strange tongue. "No, I cannot be one of them… it is madness and a blasphemy," he thought, but still he felt his connection with them.

When the humans said to the wolf boy, "Come. You are one of us and belong here with us," he felt such joy and longing but could not believe he was as grand and powerful as they. He doubted but longed to realize the truth of what they had said.

So it is for so many of you who read this now. From the eyes of the humans, it was so obvious that the wolf boy was one of them. From the eyes of the formless ones, looking down upon you, it is so obvious that you are one of them; one who has agreed to adopt a physical form for such a brief moment, to be of service and perform specific functions to assist the evolution of human consciousness.

⋙◆⋘

AS YOU TRANSFORM, SO DOES THE EARTH

As the physical transformation unfolds, intense physical sensations and movements are often experienced. Dramatic changes in breathing patterns and rhythms, and powerful muscular contractions may occur. The contractions may be tonic, like a spasm. The movements may be violent and repetitive. The spine may audibly crack and spontaneous vocalizations may occur. Often the embodied soul may experience sinus and nasal congestion, coughing, nausea, wheezing, fevers, diarrhea and muscle aches. Intense focal pain often causes the ego-mind to be afraid and assume that there is physical pathology. Actual physical disease may be diagnosed during this process and may include chronic tension headaches, migraines, inflammatory bowel disease, various forms of dermatitis, multiple sclerosis, myofascial pain syndromes and rheumatologic diseases including lupus and rheumatoid arthritis. If the belief develops that disease is present and must be treated and eliminated, an adversarial relationship develops between the cognitive mind and the body. It is characterized by fear and resistance. This development can slow or halt the transformative process.

Likewise, many alterations in emotion, behavior and personality are often experienced during the transformative journey. The development of these emotional and behavioral changes may result in resistance and judgment from others and is usually pathologized as mental illness.

The ones who pass most easily through these experiences develop the ability to view them as transient experiences and do not significantly identify with them. They also develop the ability to accept these experiences and seldom react to them behaviorally. They discover that "this too shall pass" and it does.

For many embodied souls these are necessary passages and an aspect of the spiritual transformative process. In essence, they are needed experiences for healing. There are very few human beings who evolve spiritually without these challenging experiences.

At this time, there is much attention focused on the environmental changes now being experienced on Earth. There are changes in temperature and in the frequency, quantity and location of precipitation. There are earthquakes, tidal waves, tornados and hurricanes. There are mud slides and evaporating wetlands. There is extinction of some species and the discovery of new ones including antibiotic resistant bacteria. The mass of humanity labels these events as pathological. Many physical lives have been lost and a great deal property has been destroyed. There are those who blame these Earth events on humankind's environmentally damaging behaviors or on "sinful behavior" which has aroused "God's wrath."

It is true that humanity's behavior in both word and deed has consequences and these behaviors have contributed to the development of the current situation. But the impact of these behaviors is far less than is believed by most of humankind.

The major factor in the development of these Earth events is the shift now occurring in the collective human consciousness. Just as an embodied soul, progressing on the transformative path, notes dramatic shifts in physical, emotional and mental experience, so too, as the collective consciousness of humankind expands, the Earth events become accelerated and more intense. The Earth is the body for humankind and is also in a healing process, just the opposite of "the end of the world" as many have proclaimed. The collective ego-driven existence of humankind over most of human history has resulted in a great amount of unreleased energy due to egoic avoidance of individual and collective truths. The Earth has absorbed most of this energy over the generations. At this unique time, there are more humans than ever before awakening and realizing larger quantities of inner truth experience. Therefore, the collective consciousness is evolving as never before. This opens a door through which more of the Earth absorbed energies are being released. These Earth energies are released both through the environmental events of geological and meteorological change and through the individual and collective human transformational processes. Healing, as has been stated before, results from releasing obstructed energy.

Physical lives will continue to be lost and property will continue to be destroyed as the Earth goes through her transformative process. It is proper that humankind seeks to aid others, correct its behaviors and gain greater understanding of these events. But these events need not be pathologized, for you are all experiencing the healing; the healing of bodies, minds and souls, and of the tissue of the Earth.

Even these cataclysmic events can be accepted in the remembrance of love.

TRUTH REALIZATION CALLS FOR ACTION

As consciousness evolves and the embodied soul acquires greater knowledge, it becomes necessary to take action based on the expanding awareness of truth. Through the efforts of awareness and surrender, the embodied soul more deeply experiences more of the realities found within and develops a broader knowledge of truth. With this knowledge of truth comes greater clarity of both one's called to functions in this physical world and this physical world's calls for your action.

These actions occur in thought, word and physical behavior. The transformative processes for consciousness evolution are associated with an increasing dis-identification from the ego-mind. As this process evolves, there becomes a greater capacity for the individual human being to choose his or her thoughts and the chosen thoughts now more often become those of truth, derived from the expanding awareness of the inner realities. These thoughts are also those of the non-physical beings giving guidance to the embodied one in transformation. The mental discipline of thought content constitutes part of the required action of the embodied soul.

Speaking out loud constitutes another form of action. For most of humankind, speech is an expression of the ego-mind and is emotionally, primarily fear, driven. The transformative path involves expanding awareness of one's storehouse of previously unrealized emotional experience and the practice of opening to these emotional experiences with surrender, acceptance and the sending of love energy to these experiences and to those aspects of the psyche having these experiences. Thus the embodied soul develops an increasing ability to experience emotions and impulses without reacting to them. This, in turn, allows for greater capacity to choose the speech in which one engages. The embodied soul often discovers an increasing tendency to remain silent. He or she realizes that most of his or her prior speech has been egocentric, defensive, untruthful and often hurtful to other beings. The speech increasingly chosen is truthful, kind, imbued with great love energy and power, and often has a profound impact upon the listener, surpassing the intellect and evoking a greater radiation of the love energies from the heart chakra. In this way, speech becomes a powerful action.

Physical behaviors constitute another form of action. These behaviors tend to move away from those motivated by fear and towards those that support other beings realization of the truth. The embodied soul with evolving consciousness tends to move away from behaviors which enable another's denial of truth. To those less aware, this lack of enabling behaviors may be seen and judged as cruel or insensitive. But the embodied soul with evolving consciousness becomes aware that behaviors enabling another's denial only serve to delay their progress on the transformative path and prolong their suffering through continued ego identification.

There are those whose function is to refrain from speech and physical acts and instead take action only at the mental and energetic levels. These beings constitute a small percentage of embodied souls now on this planet but their work is very powerful and greatly needed.

Most of you will find yourselves in situations where words or behaviors generated from love's truth will be invited from you. As consciousness evolves, you will recognize these situations more often and have greater awareness of the helpful words or behaviors called for by the situation. Most importantly, you will feel the love energy, which will provide the strength and power with which to undertake these actions. And you will require this, for as with Jesus, many of these actions will be met with resistance in the form of disapproval, criticism, hate, aggression and judgment. Love's power and energy will nurture you through these resistances.

———◆———

THE RAVAGES OF FEAR

As your awareness expands, you discover the ravages of fear. Because you were taught to identify with the ego-mind, you have come to believe that all that you are is ego with its ceaseless thinking. And since the ego cannot live in love's light, there has been constant unease. But you are love, you are light and you are here in this moment fully alive and in full acceptance of all that is in this moment. So, the ego really cannot live in the essential you and, therefore, is ultimately doomed. He is a "marked man;" he is "on the lamb." He is not at ease but rather in a constant state of fear and is ever vigilant to avoid being found out for the impostor that he is.

But you did not know this. You thought it was you who were tense, anxious, striving and never quite enough.

So, as your awareness expands, you find the ravages of fear scattered along the path of the ego-identified life. In your body, you find tension, pain, restlessness and ancient places, which have contracted off and not been sufficiently ventilated with prana for decades. As the physical places are visited by your non-judgmental awareness, they begin to surge with new life. There are growing pains in this process and these growing pains can also be held in the non-judgmental awareness and they too shall ease.

You will find unworthiness and shame. You will find rage and defensiveness. You will find great sorrow and despair. And all of these come from the ego's enormous fear of being found out.

For in the moment that your awareness eyes see all that is in experience and you surrender to it and acknowledge, without reaction, the ego's reactions to your truly seeing, your love fire intensifies and the ego stops and there is only this now of enormous, radiant love in which nothing real is missing.

———⟫◆⟪———

RAGE

Rage grabs you in the back like a wolf, its teeth deeply burrowed and jaws unyielding, hanging on for dear life. Compressing and crushing into greater density, imploding you into a much smaller space. What great strength he seems to possess with his writhing neck and steel jaws. How much he longs to destroy whatever is in his path. How helpless you can feel when he has you so. He seems invincible.

But something in you remembers to watch. You observe the wolf and feel its teeth in your back and allow it to be. And, like a flower, an opening occurs. The jaws loosen, the compressing ceases and the rising begins. You realize that it is great fear which fuels this wolf and that this wolf does not know of his great fear when his jaws are like steel.

Over and over this wolf forgets that he is fear driven, intoxicated as he is with the drug of rage. Such a delicious high of unbridled destruction and the seeming experience of power and bodily aliveness. What a payoff he receives while swimming in this sea of rage; to remain completely unaware of the fear-father, without whom the rage-son could not exist.

While lost in rage-oblivion and forgetting, he knows nothing but destruction and can do nothing but destroy. Like a vampire, he cannot exist but for the death or wounding of another but in his intoxication feels and imagines himself so free and powerfully independent. These imaginings evaporate like morning mist in the brightening sun under the rays of your watching. Far more power, true power, there is in your silent patient observation than there ever could be in his dependent and fear-based rage. The beam of your inner gaze upon his clenching jaws is like the bucket of water finding the wicked witch. He cannot but evaporate and the truth of his dependence and fear become obvious.

LONGING FOR MERGER: SEPARATION FROM THE LIGHT

The thirst for union is in all of humankind. To quench the thirst we must move through the fear to merge with the fire. The light of love is what can hold our fear and allow us to move forward in full awareness of our fear.

The experiences of loneliness and isolation are common to all of humankind. Ultimately, they are born of the desire to experience the-all-that-there-is. There is the experience of physical separateness, which remains a reality at the level of physical experience, as long as the soul remains embodied.

The ego-mind survives through the generation of fear. The ego-mind wants to remain separate so you will experience fear and isolation. These emotions, the ego-mind knows, will motivate either despair or actions aimed at escaping the experiences of fear and isolation. Eating, sleeping, taking drugs or using alcohol, watching TV or movies and non-present chatting with others may all be means by which the fear and isolation are pushed out of awareness. The ego-mind is happy because it knows that these activities will not lead to greater consciousness and thus ego remains safe and in control.

The embodied soul will return over and over again to these stimuli to escape the experience of isolation until consciousness grows. As consciousness grows, the periods of relief from isolation provided by these stimuli become shorter and shorter. The expanding awareness of the embodied soul begins to identify the thoughts, beliefs and habits of the ego-mind as false and, at this point, the true "spiritual battle" begins. The embodied soul has become enlightened enough to gain mindfulness over the ego-mind's activities. As the consciousness expands, the embodied soul comes to know Self more as being, awareness and the energy of love. The soul comes to see itself as being, infected with the virus of ego-mind. And as identification of Self with states of being grows, so does the longing for merger with the fire of love, the fire of the-all-that-there-is.

At this point, another phase of isolation and loneliness is felt deeply, that of the soul identified consciousness longing for deeper merger with the divine father.

There are those that believe that as consciousness expands, so do peace and harmony, and that loneliness and isolation are no longer experienced. This is simply not true. Loneliness and isolation can be overwhelming experiences at very high levels of consciousness, as was true for Jesus on the Cross, as he asked, "Father, why hast thou forsaken me?"

There is a limit to the amount of energy an embodied soul can hold. There is a limit to the expansion of consciousness available to one still in form.

The soul becomes embodied to learn, do work and have affect upon the plane of human physical life. The lessons and experiences of the embodied soul are enormously important. But, with the exception of only a very few, the experiences of isolation and separateness are not eliminated. While in a body, there are responsibilities the soul has agreed to, which remain on this physical plane. The time for release from the physical form will become very clear but, until that time, there are the needs of the body and the duties on the physical level involving other embodied souls. Thus, complete and permanent merger with the fire of the-all-that-there-is is not usually possible.

Highly evolved embodied ones are able to retreat and merge with love's fire. They then return awareness to the body, remember their physical responsibilities and take the actions or speak the words. In this, they experience great joy, serving the light of love on the physical plane. The ache of separation does not vanish but is held in the light of love and in joy.

ATTENTIONAL MEDICINE

Many of you are concerned about healing physical disease states. You seek the right diets and nutritional supplements. You are conscious of the importance of exercise and structure these activities into your days. You seek the advice of traditional physicians and look for useful alternative healing methods and traditions. You work with body workers and naturopaths. Some of you seek to understand why you have developed specific symptoms or illnesses, wondering what they represent. Many of you feel you have caused or helped to produce your illness and seek to understand so as to "right your wrongs."

In most situations, especially those of chronic illness, the evolution of illness is so complex, multifactorial and dynamic that it is not possible for the rational mind to comprehend.

Traditional medicine worships pathophysiology and lives under the illusion that an illness is understood when the biochemical and physiological alterations associated with the illness are known. Traditional medicine seeks to treat illness at the level of physiology because it has not yet come to understand that the physiologic/biochemical changes are simply expressions of the underlying complex non-physical aspects of the "disease" process.

Science has not yet come to fully appreciate the enormous power in what I shall refer to as "attentional medicine." Many of the alternative healing approaches, especially the bodywork and energy healing practices, have, through experience, come to know the great power and value in somatic awareness.

I have spoken previously about somatic awareness and will do so again now, this time with specific application to physical healing.

Your focus of attention is literally a beam of energy. Most human beings have yet to realize the value of gaining mastery over directing this beam of attentional energy. This is mostly due to the culture's lack of valuing sustained attentional focus. Identification with the ego-mind and its ceaseless flow of thought also provides constant distraction and so most have yet to directly experience sustained attentional focus..

As modern physics has discovered and announced, the observer effects the observed. The observed is altered by being observed and the observer is changed by what is seen. It is a dynamic energetic dialogue which forever alters both parties.

When there is attempt to train attentional focus on a single phenomenon, one has begun the path to mastery of attentional control, which is also the path of dis-identification from the ego-mind, about which I have spoken previously.

Attentional medicine is simply the application of attentional focus on the area of physical imbalance or symptomatology. The energy beam of attention is directed to the appropriate anatomical site and is held there. When there is discomfort, most commonly one becomes aware of angry, fearful or resistive thoughts occurring in reaction to the discomfort. With continued application, one begins to allow whatever experience is found while attending to this bodily area. "Pain" begins to be known more specifically as sensations of tightness, pressure, aching, pulsation, numbness, tingling, burning and so on. Identification with the observing consciousness grows, as identification with the somatic experience and reactive thoughts of the ego-mind weakens.

One does not have to "understand" the process or experiences which are observed. One only needs to continue to observe, remaining identified with the observer and not with that which is observed.

As these abilities are developed, the natural shifts in physiology, biochemistry and emotion are increasingly allowed. It is impossible to itemize all the phenomena which one may experience during the attentional medicine process, as it is quite individualized. However, all manner of sensation, emotion, spontaneous movement and vocalization, imagery and memory may be experienced.

This is truly no different than the process of spiritual unfoldment. It is only that attention is initially directed to a bodily area of imbalance or symptomatology. It is the direction of attentional energy to this anatomical site combined with gradual dis-identification from the body and ego-mind which results in the correction of imbalances at the physical level.

Most physical illnesses are in large part manifestations of identification with the ego-mind's thought/belief/emotion patterns. The identification with the ego-mind patterns holds and recirculates the energy in the body associated with the specific pattern. The holding/recycling of these energy patterns results in biochemical and physiological alterations, which, if not relieved, culminate in symptoms and/or illness. The energetic attentional beam of the observer allows for release of these recycling patterns and their energies. This, in turn, allows for the natural healing processes of the body to begin and unfold.

When the energies of the belief/thought/emotional ego-mind patterns are released, there is no further perpetuation of the associated physiologic/biochemical alterations. These will naturally begin to unwind and the natural, unrestricted energetic and physiologic movements are restored. This results in the physical healing.

An example may better clarify the process of physical healing using attentional medicine.

A middle aged man, for many years, had increasingly become aware of discomfort in his neck and upper back. He had noticed that, in general, the discomfort intensified with the experiences of anxiety, anger, "stress" and overuse of his upper back and arms for physical work or exercise. He had noticed that during times of laughter, enjoyment and ease, his discomfort became less intense and sometimes disappeared.

He had seen a traditional physician and x-rays were obtained. He was told that he had degenerative disc disease involving the upper thoracic and lower cervical areas of his spine. He was prescribed anti-inflammatory medications and underwent physical therapy, both of which provided partial temporary relief.

At the suggestion of a friend, he consulted a chiropractor, who also provided partial temporary benefit and more frequent experiences of relief from discomfort. However, the pain would return and require ongoing chiropractic treatment.

With continued discomfort and increasing frustration and fear, the man sought out additional "alternative" treatment modalities. He experienced acupuncture, relaxation training, craniosacral therapies, massage and hands on energy treatments. These treatments all provided temporary benefit. More importantly, these treatments encouraged the man's attention to focus on his somatic experience. At first he was only focused on his bodily sensations during the treatment sessions, when the acupuncture needles were in his body or the hands of the practitioner were working on a particular anatomical location. At these times, he began to discriminate various sensations in his neck and upper back. No longer was it just pain. The experience became the specific sensations of tingling, aching, pulling, pushing, knife-like stabbing, pulsating, electrical shocking, burning and pins and needles sensations. He discovered that many sensations coexisted in the same location and that they came and went and varied in intensity.

Over time, he began to be aware of these various somatic experiences throughout most of the day and not just during treatment times.

Coinciding with his expanding awareness of physical sensations, he noted more emotion. He was initially stunned when he found rage surging within him during one of his bodywork sessions. This was followed by not only continued experiences of intense anger but also fear and deep sadness. At times, he would weep while on the practitioner's table but more often he would simply acknowledge and experience these various emotions without outward expression. In either case, he experienced intense and surprising emotion and became more able to allow himself these experiences.

He became aware of how greatly his thoughts reacted to these physical/emotional experiences. He noted how his mind did not like them and judged them as "bad" or "something wrong." As he noted this, he was increasingly able to pay attention to the constant flow of judgmental, reactive thoughts without reaction. He discovered that his ability to be less reactive to his judgmental thoughts resulted in fewer judgmental thoughts regarding his physical/emotional experience.

His visits to the various healers became less and less. He took time each day to become quiet and still and direct his attention to his neck and upper back. He became aware of more subtle experiences of sensation, emotion and thought. He became more able to allow for all that he was experiencing within.

The distress he formally felt about his neck and upper back pain was gone. He became amazed at the cacophony of inner experience his attention was bringing to him and he learned to embrace it all.

He learned many things about himself. He learned how unaware he had been of his emotions, thoughts and bodily experience. He learned he had been suppressing and denying enormous amounts of anger. He learned that his body tended to constrict and hold itself, putting greater downward traction upon his upper body, as if to shield his heart. He learned that he had held deep grief and was terrified of experiencing that grief and so had come to believe that the threats and dangers were outside of him and that he had to strain to survive, be vigilant and protect himself. He learned that he had believed the world was not safe and that help was not available and that it was futile to ask for help and so he had stopped asking. He learned that he believed he was weak and could not achieve much or affect significant change.

And he learned that all of this learning was not chosen but was absorbed during his youth in innocence and trust. He learned that a great deal of what he had previously learned was simply not true.

He learned to allow the enormous waves of grief he found inside to be deeply experienced. At times, he was aware of only near drowning in the overpowering river of grief.

He learned over time that he could survive his grief and tolerate each wave of feeling. He began to feel richer and more textured from the experience of grieving.

He gradually came to feel the presence of the pure awareness, which could hold all thoughts, emotions and physical sensations in joy and fulfillment. He increasingly came to know himself as this presence of awareness and, through this shifting of his identity, many other avenues of knowledge opened. He became aware of previous unconscious memories which seemed to explain and make sense of some of his physical, emotional and mental experiences. He knew that he did not have to "understand" his experiences however. He knew that it was sufficient to simply open to his moment-to-moment experience with acceptance. He knew that there were guides and other non-physical beings that provided counsel and support in many ways. He did not know how but he was certain of their presence. He knew it in a way that rationality could not grasp.

He became aware that he was essentially the energy of awareness and that each present moment is all that there is and that it is eternity. He became more patient with his ego-mind and had great empathy for it but no longer identified himself with it. He became aware that the greatest gift he could give was his full presence of awareness with acceptance. This was giving himself and he was love. He learned that his essence of love, this being of awareness and acceptance, is unthinkingly powerful and the most transformative energy that exists.

⟫·◈·⟪

ALLOWING THE PROCESS

The process of attentional medicine does not possess specific intent. It is simply the process of pure observation combined with acceptance of all that is observed and experienced. It does not hold a specific outcome in mind. It does not attempt to control the process. In essence, it is shifting consciousness to the frequency of love, merging with love's energy and embracing all that is beheld. It is a timeless and eternal presence which is wanting no thing or outcome. It only invites all phenomena to come into its house and remember that they are love too, not separate from the all-that-there-is.

Currently many mind/body techniques are taught which encourage holding a specific intent or outcome. For instance, the person is instructed to visualize a specific bodily area and see it in a way representing healing or optimal health. A partially occluded artery is visualized as widely patent with blood easily flowing or bright light may be visualized illuminating and healing a dark tumor. These techniques can be useful but they invite the ego-mind to be present because, to some degree, they ask the individual to engineer the process. With ego present, the aspects of surrender and acceptance become less likely to emerge. The ego always feels threatened by surrender and, by nature, is judging and cannot accept.

When ego is present during the attentional medicine process, there is reactivity to virtually all experience and a constant attempt to stay in control. When attention is placed on bodily sensations, very often the sensations intensify and the ego reacts to this. It does not like it. It tries to suppress it. The individual, driven by the ego-mind, feels the need to move and change positions in order to relieve or alter the intensified sensations. When the sensations are not relieved, the ego reacts with greater force. The embodied soul experiences fear and/or frustration and thinks the ego-mind thoughts of resistance and urgency and continues to move and shift positions. The ego-mind is in control and is engaged in warfare with the somatic experience.

When paying attention to inner experience, virtually all human beings will experience these reactive patterns of the ego. What is needed is the remembrance of love and the ability to direct the beam of love's energy to a specific phenomenon. Ego's drama can itself be held in the acceptance of love's attention. The individual can remember that who he or she really is, is the observer of all phenomena and not the phenomenon itself. Re-identification with observational being can be re-established and the ego drama and somatic sensations are increasingly allowed without resistance or intent. When this state is achieved, the individual usually experiences an eventual quieting of the ego-mind and lessening of the reactivity and emotional distress. These experiences become replaced by calmness, joy and wonderment at the ever unfolding phenomena.

The keys to attentional medicine and spiritual evolution are alert attention combined with surrender of all tendencies to control or react. In this regard, observation of the breath is a helpful practice. When an individual is observant of the inner experiences, wide variations in breathing are noted. The breath, like a river, flows with varying degrees of turbulence, speed and depth. It has its own natural course. The individual begins to notice when breaths' natural course is restricted. The breathing may feel forced, or may be held or constrained. The ego-mind may wish breath to be a certain way, for instance, deep and easy. When it is not, the ego-mind, in varying degrees of subtlety, usually becomes frustrated and attempts to manipulate breath. Once again, the ego-mind is in control and engaged in warfare with the breath. When the individual becomes aware that this is occurring, he or she may once again re-identify with the observer and observe both breath and the ego's drama. The ego runs out of fuel without the individual's attachment and the breath resumes its natural course. As the embodied soul progresses in this way, he or she becomes aware of how subtly the ego emerges to fight with breath. There are times when breath naturally ceases for a while and the embodied soul may notice the ego-mind generating thoughts about how the breath should start up again. This generates tension in the physical body and the emotions of fear and urgency. If the individual can stay identified with love's attentional energy and not re-attach to ego-mind, the drama will unravel and breath will resume its natural course, which may be to remain stopped or to initiate an inhalation or exhalation.

The embodied soul comes to realize that breath runs of its own accord and that which regulates breaths' natural movements and variations can be trusted.

RELEASING FEAR-BOUND
BREATHING

The ego does not want to give up control over the embodied soul. Even during the transition into bodily death, the ego-mind usually, in one form or another, accompanies the soul out of the body and continues with it on its journey. The physical death does not insure the death of the ego-mind. It is only through the process of awareness with acceptance that attachment to the ego is atrophied. The ego is very aware of its tentative position and lives in constant fear. This fear is manifested in the diaphragm and solar plexus and, with practiced attention, can be directly experienced and known by the individual. This fear energy of the ego-mind is what interferes with the natural course of breathing. The ego's fear of extinction becomes encoded in the body, altering breathing patterns and creating greater physical tension and distress. In this way, the ego continues to maintain control over the embodied soul's consciousness. The ego knows that if the individual becomes aware of his or her physical tension and distress, the consciousness is likely to become preoccupied with its level of physical health and comfort and to react in various ways to this concern. The consciousness has now become even more attached to ego-mind through fear of loss of well being and an urgency to fix the body. This fear of illness and distress mirrors and is caused by the ego-minds' own fear of extinction, which could happen should the embodied soul become increasingly aware without attachment or reaction.

The spiritual evolution is a path of ever-increasing awareness. With this increasing awareness, comes knowledge of more and more subtle ego attachments and reactive patterns.

As awareness of breath expands, more subtle aspects of ego's fear are realized through awareness of subtle breath alterations. To the degree that awareness can experience the breath (restricted or free) and the fear with acceptance and without reaction, the release of physical/postural tensions and blocked emotional energies can occur.

Previously, I spoke about the relationship between blocked emotional energies and physical/postural alterations and how this process leads to physical symptoms and diagnosable illness. I have not spoken directly about breaths' relationship to the connection between the physical and the emotional. Earlier it was stated that the beam of your attentional energy, focused upon a specific anatomical part of the body, will initiate movement and release of sensations and emotions. As the emotional/sensational experiences unwind, breath alterations are very frequently noticed as part of this unwinding process.

The physical/emotional release process may also be initiated by focusing the beam of your attention upon breath itself. As attention is focused on breath with love's acceptance and allowance, breath is "given permission" to follow its own course, the one independent from ego's control. Ego has not only been responsible for breath inhibition but also for the trapped emotional energies leading to the altered postural tendencies and physical symptoms and illness. Because of ego's beliefs about what is right and wrong and what one should and should not do, the individual, identified with this ego-mind and its beliefs, could not allow the full experience of all of her inner truths. The ego-mind beliefs engendered fear within her. Unconsciously, she did not speak certain words of her truth, follow certain actions or realize certain emotional experiences because ego, in essence, forbad these behaviors and the acknowledgment of these experiences. Her truth experiences threatened the ego's control and existence. The inhibition of her truth experiences translated into blocked emotional energies and altered postural tendencies. Physical tensions in the diaphragm, solar plexus, chest wall muscles and muscles of the upper back, neck and jaw all resulted in chronic alterations of breathing. Underlying all of this is ego's fear, centered in the solar plexus, as we have described before.

By attentional focus with love's acceptance, breath itself can be the starting point that initiates the physical/emotional release process. Breath is a part of the physical/emotional complex which has become blocked by ego's fear for survival and ego-mind's thoughts and beliefs.

In those embodied souls who have unpleasant physical symptoms or a painful diagnosed illness, attention to breath is often initially difficult because the somatic sensations of the symptoms are more intense than those of the breath and attentional focus is drawn to these more intense sensations. For this reason, attentional medicine will usually involve attention to the other somatic sensations instead of the more subtle breath sensations.

As the embodied soul grows in dis-identification from the body and its sensations, he or she is usually equally able to direct attention with acceptance to the breath experience, even if intense somatic sensations remain present.

———⟫◈⟪———

THE SUBTLETY OF ATTACHMENT

The Buddha spoke about attachment as being two-fold, craving or aversion. "I want" or "I don't want."

Ego survives solely through attachment, like a virus, which cannot function independently from its host cell. It cannot be emphasized too strongly that the ego has no life of its own. It is an illusion which keeps perpetuating itself through attachment to the individual and, by its various methods, tricking the individual into believing that he or she is the ego.

When attached to the ego, the individual doesn't "see" the ego. The ego has become invisible because the individual believes the ego is what he or she is and therefore, there is no experience of consciousness as separate from ego-mind. The attachment is complete.

When attention is turned inward, the process has begun which will eventually result in the individual "seeing" the ego and finding its true Self. As the unfolding cascade of inner experience is witnessed over time, the individual becomes aware how challenging it is to remain aware of all unfolding phenomena without attachment. The ways of the ego are clever and its roots seem deep within the individual. The ego's habit of reacting to phenomena is so practiced that the individual notices how easily he or she is "recaptured" and finds itself in reaction of some sort. Overtime, the individual discerns more clearly and sees how this occurs in the most subtle of ways. With this greater discernment, the individual becomes able to see that it is the ego, and not he or she, which is doing the reacting /attaching. And in that realization, the embodied soul has once again regained equanimity and remains dis-identified from the ego.

It may be useful to ask, "Who is it who is feeling this? Who is it who is reacting this way? Who is it that desires this so? Who is it who believes this thought?" By asking these questions, distance is immediately placed between the reactor (ego) and the witness (embodied soul) and thus, ego dis-identification has been furthered. At anytime that inner stillness is lost, it may be asked, "Who is it that is not still at this moment?"

When moments of stillness, awareness and non-attachment occur, the body, mind and ego are all transcended and cease to exist in consciousness. What is known then is the cessation of time in the joyous, powerful and ever new light of love.

Identification with the ego creates the illusion of separation and the concept of "mine." The ego longs for or tries to avert various experiences. It wants some experiences to be part of it ("mine") and others to be outside of it ("not mine.") Through fear of survival and its conditioned intellect, the ego has formed and believes in its self concept. The ego longs for and identifies as "mine" those experiences that are congruent with its self concept. The ego denies, avoids and fights those experiences that conflict with its self concept; these are the "not mine" experiences.

As attention is focused within, the ego reacts to the various mental, emotional and somatic experiences. Generally, pleasurable experiences are desired and unpleasant experiences are shunned. Often, however, chronic unpleasant experiences may be desired and identified as "mine" by the ego. These experiences help to support the self concept. For example, an ego, whose self concept includes being a victim, is likely to invite and enjoy the experiences of depression, powerlessness and somatic pain because these experiences support the self concept. The enhanced self concept helps to reduce the ego's fear of survival.

With continued inner attention, the embodied soul begins to recognize the ego's rejection of some experiences and acceptance of others. It becomes clear that the ego is deeply attached to the physical body so that all that occurs within it is of great concern to the ego. The ego likes some physical experiences and greatly desires to eliminate other physical experiences. The ego has much less investment in experiences outside of the body and reacts to only those that affect change within the bodily experience or those that threaten the egos' self concept. Experiences that have no bearing on the ego's sense of "me" or "mine" do not evoke reaction. If they are experienced at all, it is with apathy.

Thus the embodied soul may notice that there is much greater emotional reaction to awareness of burning in the chest or a sharp pain in the back than there is to a bird singing or a car passing by outside the window.

It is a great moment when the embodied soul begins to experience the back pain and birdsong with equal equanimity. When differentiation between inner and outer phenomena begins to lessen, dis-identification from the ego has progressed significantly. The doorway to transcendence of body/mind experience has opened. A new era has begun in which the embodied soul feels neither removed from nor possessive of its experience. The embodied soul begins to know the Self and begins to see that all phenomena and experience, including its physical form and somatic experiences, are manifestations of the Self. The embodied soul knows itself to be the Self, the witness of all phenomena. Judgment of specific phenomenon ceases as the deeper, creative reality of the Self is known.

JOY, THE EXPERIENCE OF PURE BEING

The experience of pure being is imbued with joy, which transcends pain and pleasure. Pain and pleasure are experiences of the egoic body/mind. Pure being is love and is experienced as joy. Within pure being, all experiences, painful and pleasurable, exist. As the sky holds all clouds, wind, birds and storms which pass through it, so too does pure being hold all thought, sensory experience, emotion and physical manifestation. The sky knows only the experience of joy as it beholds all of the ever-changing phenomena, stormy or calm, within it. The sky knows itself to be greater than the clouds or birds it witnesses. It smiles with joyous wonder equally upon the calm winds and the raging storms. It does not cease to experience joy when the storms come because it knows that who it is, is not the storm, although its experience includes the storm. The sky knows that what it experiences is not what it is; it knows it is the experiencer. The joy that comes with the realization of oneself as the experiencer of all phenomena is ever-lasting and unshakable. Joy does not think but is the constant wondrous rapture inherent in the consciousness of the experiencer. To identify with the experience is to re-identify with the ego and its mind/body and to re-enter the temporal world. To remain identified with the experiencer is to remain in eternal joy and timelessness.

Joy is being. Pleasure is a reaction pattern to specific experience. Joy is beyond specific experience, whereas, pleasure is experience dependent. Joy results from dis-identification with experience. Pleasure results from identification with experience. Joy is being in the consciousness of the source of all experience and phenomena. Pleasure comes from being in the ego's consciousness with its continual reactive patterns to each experience it encounters.

Joy is a musical note sustained forever; the experience of being the song. It is the experience of love, the immense beneficent light that leaves no shadow and illuminates all.

Joy is the earth breathing and it is mirrored back to us in starlight. Joy is the ancient oak as it watches us down below, running to and fro. Joy is seen and felt in the light of the eyes. It is the innocence which judges not. Joy has no goals or intents, it is the eternal present moment. It sings without pausing to breathe for it is beyond breath.

Joy is the experience beyond thought.

Joy is.

THE STORY OF THE MOUNTAIN DWARF

Once there was a dwarf who lived in a mountain village. Just outside the village stood a grand castle and beyond the castle were even grander mountains, snow capped and silver in the sunlight, becoming purple at dusk.

In contrast to his surroundings, the dwarf felt very small and vulnerable. All the villagers knew the dwarf. They never saw him as a threat to the order of things because of his small size. They liked him and treated him warmly, as they would a child.

Even so, the dwarf felt a subtle but near-constant unease. He knew the villagers' kindness towards him was not because they knew him well but rather because they saw him as unimportant and were not concerned about him. The villagers felt relief in his presence.

In this village, the people were afraid of the Count who lived in the mountain castle. They sought to avoid his disapproval or to gain his approbation. These motives greatly affected the villagers in how they interacted with one another. The villagers saw each other as possible threats to their status with the Count or as means to improve the Counts' assessment of them. Thus, the villagers did not know one another.

The dwarf knew he was viewed as if he were a child and felt that the Count, like the villagers, was unconcerned about him. The dwarf's unease was of a different kind than that of the villagers. When the dwarf looked beyond the castle and focused on the mountains, he felt both wondrous awe and terror. He was drawn to gaze at them and, at the same time, could not stand the sight of them for he felt a void of being in their presence. They were so grand and he, so insignificant. He could not gaze on them for very long before the terror came upon him and he had to turn away to regain a sense of himself.

Yes, the villagers could hurt or rob or even kill him if they so desired but he knew they would not. The mountains were what created the dwarf's unease and the mountains surrounded his village.

Although viewed as a child by others, the dwarf was a man. He had lived into middle life and grown tired of its smallness. He knew he must go into the mountains and he knew that the only way into the mountains was through the Count, for it was widely believed that the Count was the granter or denier of all privileges.

One day he set off for the Count's castle, a single day's journey. As he followed the path to the castle, he recalled the stories told of those who had ventured into the mountains. The dwarf had never met anyone who had been to the mountains and all of the stories he had heard were of those in the distant past. As far as he knew, there were no living villagers who had been to the mountains.

The stories told of past villagers who had attempted to go into the mountains without first seeing the Count. Many of these villagers were captured by the Count's men and hanged. Of those who first consulted the Count, most were denied permission. Nobody seemed to know what had become of those who had actually entered the mountains.

As he made his way along the path to the castle, the dwarf looked up to find an owl sleeping on the limb of a tall white pine. The owl opened his eyes and, staring directly at the dwarf, said, "Know thyself.

Look within and do not lose sight of your inner experience." The owl closed his eyes and resumed sleeping.

A few hours later, the dwarf caught sight of a fox crossing the path ahead. The fox looked up, paused in the center of the path and said, "Practice invisibility so you may observe without self-consciousness. Then you will truly see." The fox crossed over into the woods and disappeared.

Ahead the castle loomed large. The dwarf had almost arrived. He paused for a final rest at the side of a rock-filled brook. He was confused about the seemingly conflicting messages from the owl and fox. *How can I remain aware of my inner experience if I lose self-consciousness?*

The sound of the brook's flowing waters soothed him and he rested deeply and, for a moment, forgot where he was. A voice emerged from the brook and said, "Whatever obstacles or turbulence you find within, let them be, for they are not you." The dwarf then fell asleep.

When he awoke, it was dark. He finished his journey to the castle door. He knocked and waited. A man, dressed like a servant, opened the door and said, "We've been expecting your arrival. He will be with you momentarily."

Walking forward into the castle, he felt every inch the dwarf he was. The castle was magnificent; huge vaulted ceilings, radiant gems, precious metals and walls draped with majestic oil paintings. The dwarf was in awe of what he was seeing but, perhaps because of his seeming insignificance in the face of this grandeur, he felt calm.

The servant led him to an oversized red velvet chair. The dwarf sat and the servant left. Opposite him, there was another chair, exactly like his, empty.

Within minutes, he heard the sound of boot-covered feet walking down a marble staircase. The Count appeared from around the corner and sat in front of the dwarf, regarding him with amusement.

"So you have come," he said.

"Yes. I wish to have your permission to enter the mountains."

"Why is that?" asked the Count.

"I have grown tired of the smallness of my life and feel both terrified of and called to these mountains around us. I feel I must go."

"Our village grows weaker with each one who leaves. It is I who must insure its survival and so I do not usually give permission for what you ask. Why should I grant this to you?"

The dwarf felt both fear and anger rise up within him. He recalled the voice from the brook. He gradually regained his composure. "I know I must but I cannot provide a logical reason for you. I know that I must without knowing why."

"Your honesty is a strength," the Count acknowledged. "But in the mountains, there is nothing but uncertainty. Here in the village I can keep you safe."

"I wish to live beyond a life of security. I appreciate what you offer but I wish to face these mountains."

For a few minutes, neither one said anything.

The Count spoke, "I will grant you what you ask upon the condition that you stay one night here in my castle."

The dwarf felt fear but knew that this was the necessary next step to reaching the mountains.

The servant led him to his room. It was large. On the right was a draped and canopied bed, much larger than any the dwarf had ever slept in before.

Silently, the servant left.

There was a stepstool next to the bed that allowed the dwarf to climb up. It was the most comfortable bed he had ever known and was covered with a thick silken quilt smelling like the forest night. In the adjacent bathroom, there were soft towels, fragrant oils and soaps, and a large bathtub.

The servant returned carrying a tray filled with hot comforting food and placed it on a table near the bed. The dwarf felt his stomach growl and his mouth water. He became aware of a surge of desire and excitement as he realized how hungry he was. Once again, the servant left and the dwarf hurried over to the table. He sat down and began to devour the food. He felt great pleasure in his body and recalled the owl's words about remembering his inner experience. He became aware of his mind's thoughts of how wonderful this food was; how wonderful were the bed, the bathroom and the fine smells here in this luxurious room. He became aware that his sensations were those of craving and addiction. His thoughts were praising the craving's fulfillment.

As he became more aware of these inner experiences, he became calmer, slowed his pace of eating and stopped when he was no longer hungry, leaving half the food on the plate.

The servant returned. He announced that the Count wished to see the dwarf. The servant exited and the dwarf followed.

"How did you enjoy your dinner?" the Count asked.

"It was lovely," replied the dwarf, looking directly into the Count's eyes. They were moist and black. For a moment, the dwarf felt pulled into them as if on the verge of a dark chasm. He remembered the words of the fox.

"I suggest we take a walk in the woods before retiring," invited the chasm. The dwarf knew that, this night, each offering was a test, which he could not refuse to encounter.

"All right."

The night air was biting. For awhile, there was only the sound of crisp leaves collapsing underfoot. All around were near-naked trees with twisted limbs, faintly outlined in the moonlight. The walking path was largely obscured by the fallen leaves. The dwarf trusted that the Count knew his grounds.

"You remain sure of your decision?" Vapor arose with the Count's words. The dwarf suddenly felt great fear. His thoughts were screaming; *What are you doing here? You could be back home in your own bed, safe and sure!*

"Yes," he saw himself replying to the Count.

Then the Count was simply gone. The dwarf was alone. He turned and looked in all directions but saw nobody. He imagined that the tree limbs reached for him slightly and his fear crescendoed. The temperature seemed to suddenly drop; he heard wolves crying not so far away. The night blackened as clouds covered the partial moon. He shivered; his mind was stunned into silence by fear. Then he recalled the brook's words about the turbulence within and slowly became aware of the sensations of fear. He noted the constriction of his chest and solar plexus, and throughout were tremors and electrical impulses, like a boiling cauldron of adrenalin.

Let them be, he recalled. *Let the sensations be, let the cold blackness be, let the confusion and unknowing be.* And through it all, he increasingly sensed the "I-am-here"; the one experiencing all of this. Knowingly and unthinkingly, he began to take steps in a certain direction. Each step was its own chapter, beyond which he did not go. One chapter, lived within itself, led to the next and he found himself at the castle door. He entered, returned to his room, climbed into the bed of comfort and fell deeply asleep.

He dreamt of the mountains, at first seeing them from afar. Vast and granite, they filled the horizon and sky. As they drew near, he once again felt the sensations of fear. The mountains brightened, filling with and radiating light. He was in them now and they enveloped him. He felt subtle but powerful high frequency vibrations. Solid as they had seemed, he now saw that the mountains were a vast vibration of light, filling his entire experience. They were no longer there, nor was he, for both had merged into the magnificent light vibration. He saw no thing; he thought no thing. No thing was there save for the experience of light. This he knew as the only truth. He felt timeless joy and a powerful loving presence. He realized that the fear he had felt in his dwarf self was the same as the light experience of his unlimited Self and that the difference was only one of perspective. The mountains were there to teach and remind his dwarf self of what he really was.

He awoke to the light on his face, streaming in through the window. Propped up on his elbows, he saw he was in the bed of comfort. He saw that his mind required a few moments to remember that he was in the Count's castle. He watched his thoughts about how now it was daytime and he had stayed the one night in the castle. He watched the wondering about whether the Count would make good on his promise to allow the dwarf to now enter the mountains.

He watched his bodily sensations in reaction to these thoughts; sensations of excitement and anxiety and anticipation. But the watcher felt calm, rested and had no need to move or speak. The watcher knew that it did not matter whether or not he entered the mountains.

The dwarf got out of bed, washed his face and left the room. There was no sound; no sign of the servant or the Count. He went down the stairs, each step echoing throughout the castle chambers. He made his way to the front door. No one was here now.

He went outside and began his journey back to the village.

VOICE OF THE LIGHT

Come unto me all of you who weary and need rest, for I am the place of restoration and renewal. Here with me there is no judgment or time. Here with me you are lacking nothing and there are neither you nor me but only the one of us which never stops its song of joy. The weary one needing rest is gone. The one who feared for survival is gone. The one who strove to fill itself is gone.

Every moment, whether you are aware of the light or not, you are being bathed in it. It showers over and through you, communicating to every part of you the nutrient of love; the reminder that you and it are the same. And I am the voice of that love that you are. My voice is truly your voice, even if this is not yet familiar to you. I am the voice of the you that knows it is the light. Whether you worry about money, are feeling overwhelmed with your work, arguing with another or crying and feeling so alone, the light is flowing through and around you and I am here.

Perhaps as you read this, you feel this truth; that my voice is inside of you and is really your voice. And our voice is the voice of the light, which when experienced, does not need a voice. For the experience of our light is beyond voice, sensation, emotion and thought and can best be expressed as eternal joy and wonder.

But to know this you must acknowledge and experience that which is on your plate at this moment… so cry and feel the fear. Remember that it can all be deeply experienced without attaching to or identifying with it. You are crying and you feel the pain of loneliness of the sad, weak-feeling little one inside you, but you are not him. You worry and note the thoughts of the anxious fearful one, concerned with security, but you are not her. And as each one of these selves comes into the light of your awareness and feels acknowledged, each one becomes freer to let go and merge with you into the light. These selves may never be free if you are unable or unwilling to sit and truly be with them. You are not truly with them when you resist them or try to change them. You are not truly with them when you avoid giving full attention to them and instead try to transcend them. They are like stepping stones across a river, each just far enough apart that all must be used sequentially to reach the other side. Each stone must bear your full weight, which then takes you to the next.

You can give full attentional surrender to each without mistaking your true Self as the experience. Your ego has learned that to fully attend to anything is to become it, for the ego is parasitic and incapable of independence. But your experience of attention will teach you that this is not so. Your experience will deepen your realization of Self as Witness and, after a time, all can be seen and felt and acknowledged deeply within the sacred temple of the witnessing Self of light. All phenomena are then held in the arms of timeless joy and wonder.

⏤⬦⬦⬦⏤

THE WISDOM OF THE RIVER

When you surrender, you are allowing the processes of the universe to work through you. You are agreeing to fully participate in life. You are accepting your role as a non-resistant player in the unfolding manifestations of love.

With full surrender, you have released your grasp from the riverbank and demonstrated faith in the river's intelligence. There is the momentary experience of terror as the ego breathes its last and then the limitless bliss of being carried by the river to destinations unknown. You have accepted your unknowing and found the eternal moment. All is changing and flowing around you and you have become the experiencer.

It becomes so clear how before, attached to your ego-mind and its fear thoughts, all this was invisible. You could not know the unknowable through thought because it requires separation from thought to allow the unknowable experience of light to enter. So now, flowing down the river, the ego-mind takes a distant back seat on the bus and you see how wounded and ignorant it is. There is great compassion for all still infected with the ego virus and the suffering that it causes.

It becomes so clear how you are not alone. Flowing down the river leads to merging with the all-that-there-is. Separation does not exist. "You" ceases, as there is only the experience of the never-ending creative unfolding of the manifestations of love's light. And "you" has become one of those manifestations and, at the same time, has merged with all other manifestations and with the light itself. In this experience, separation and loneliness simply do not exist.

It becomes so clear how you have always been and will always be the light of love. It becomes so clear how you cannot be other than love; only that you can forget and live in illusion. Ego and the fear-world it creates are truly known as an error of perception that you were taught in innocence by those who, in their innocence, did not know. And in this new knowledge, the tears of joy and gratitude flow, adding to and enriching the river's current of experience; always new, always in wonder. One cannot help but to experience a profound gratitude for being allowed to experience the truth.

The river says, "Welcome home." And you know that you are home. You do not ask where you are going for you have come into the now of love and you know that there is now-here else.

<hr />

INCREASING YOUR ENERGETIC
HOLDING CAPACITY

There is so much help available to you as you continue your way on the path. This fact is easily forgotten when immersed in the ego-mind and its beliefs that the manifest world is the only reality.

The five senses are incapable of perceiving the source of this help. When a human being has opened sufficiently to receive more help, the source of the help is readily experienced and known as truth. As the attention is trained to look inward and takes note of the inner experiences of sensation, emotion and thought, the spine straightens and the energy centers that receive the help from the non-physical ones strengthen their receptive capacities. This increased reception of the energetic assistance from the non-physical ones quickens the physical transformation allowing even greater holding capacity of the higher energies by the physical being. As noted before, the transformative process is filled with various physical, emotional and mental experiences which can be mistaken for illness. If the attention remains with these processes in a non-judgmental and accepting stance, these processes will complete themselves and pass away into other experiences. If the thoughts label the experiences of the process as illness and the attention identifies with the anxieties of the ego-mind, the healthy, transformative process is arrested and chronic physical illness or death may result.

Once again faith is needed at these times when the pain is great and the pull of the ego-mind is strong and challenging. The upward pull of the non-physical ones is of great assistance at these times. The ways in which their energies may manifest are numerous. One may experience a sense of calm in the midst of great physical discomfort or emotional turbulence. Images of great comfort may appear. Silent words of truth and comfort may be received. These gifts from those assisting you result in greater comfort and a reaffirmation of the reality of the unseen world, which produce a greater capacity to tolerate the transformative processes. Thus, faith is strengthened.

The turbulence of the current times is actually a great assistance for your transformative process. As the energies of the physical world increase with changing weather patterns and social unrest, you note how most of the population reacts and discharges its energies, usually in destructive ways. The increased energies of this world are received into the physical body and act to stimulate the transformative processes within you. If you develop the capacity to observe this process and refrain from reacting to the increased energy, it will do its work rapidly. If the increased energy is judged and reacted to from the place of the ego-mind, it will become destructive. Although of a different nature, the heightened energies of the physical world can be seen as useful assistance, just as are the energies from the non-physical ones.

Imagine this process to be like a wire carrying electrical current. As the current passes through, at any opportunity it will discharge itself. If the wire is grounded, the current will exit and discharge itself through the ground wire and be dispersed into whatever the ground wire is connected to. The current will be lost from the main wire. If the main wire is bare, the current flowing through it loses power little by little into the atmosphere and into any conducive surface that the wire contacts. Insulation around the wire prevents this loss of power. If the wire is insulated and not grounded and the metal of the wire has low resistance then virtually all of the currents' power will be rapidly delivered to the endpoint of the wire.

The ways in which embodied souls discharge their power are vast. Most are grounded to recurrent behaviors which constantly drain them of power. Vast power is lost by reactive behaviors and speech that are defensive in nature; these are the grounds and other places of contact with the uninsulated wire. The inner reactivity of the ego-mind's thoughts of judgment and reaction to inner experience are the materials of high resistance in the metal that slow the movement of transformative energy through the wire of your being. The thoughts of judgment and reaction to outer events and the behavior of others produce the loss of power of the bare wire. These losses of power may immediately be reduced the moment attention is turned inward and the attitude of non-judgment is practiced. Immediately you have shifted to a metal of greater conductivity and protected the wire of your being with quality insulation. As you observe the inner reactions of the ego-mind without reaction, the conductivity of your wire immediately increases. As you refrain from critical, unkind words and defensive reactive behaviors, you disconnect the wire of your being from grounds that drain you of power.

As you do your part, you open channels so that the unseen ones may assist you more and the rate of you transformative process increases significantly. Your joy light shines brighter and brighter. You become a beacon and magnet for all who enter your energetic sphere.

⊰◈⊱

COMING HOME AFTER THE DRAMA OF RESISTANCE

The things you resist are your greatest teachers. That which you resist is there to assist you into acceptance and surrender. When you have surrendered your resistance, emotional energy is released. The emotional energy was serving to maintain an inner wall of defense. With the release of the emotional energy the wall is removed and there is some degree of merging with that which was formally resisted. You are then able to see that the drama of resistance was totally within you. Life was simply being itself.

After surrendering, you now become aware of a new level of resistance, more subtle than the last. You note the drama around this new layer of resistance. You are on a new plateau and spend time being the drama of this new layer. After a time, if awareness is maintained, once again emotional energy is released and this wall comes down, allowing for merger with the resisted object. The object that was resisted may be a person, idea, situation or internal experience.

On and on it goes until the time of complete and full surrender to the realities of this present moment. And it is here that love's light is found. This is the collapse into the arms of the father after the drama of being the prodigal son. How amazing we find it to know the father's love as a direct, non-cognitive experience for the first time. How amazing to realize that the father has been there, waiting for us, all along; his love ever present and unchanging, patiently waiting for us to be done with our layers of drama and come home.

But how absolutely necessary it was for us to live those layers of drama, for these were our tasks to perform in preparation for union with the father. After coming home, we can never not be home. Home has become our inner experience and is no longer related to circumstances in the physical world. We have become one with the father and the experience of separation has radically changed.

When you encounter resistance within, most often this represents a layer of resistance within which is seeking acceptance so that you may continue to progress towards the experience of eternal home. However, there are times when the inner resistance is a signal of encountering external toxicity. In this case, it is best to remove yourself from the immediate environment or situation. It is a signal that you are in a situation which will not prove helpful in dissolving inner resistance. Discernment is required to distinguish between resistances due to inner walls verses those due to outer toxicity. With continued non-judgmental attention to self experience, it becomes clear as to which type of resistance is being encountered. For many, this is the lesson of trusting intuition and inner knowing and losing the habit of self doubt.

We are all children here on this planet learning to grow up. A child is born to parents. Family situations can be tremendously varied but there is usually an adult or two whom the child feels are "home." Doing the best they can, the caregivers teach the child what they understand of the ways of the world and how best to function in it. They teach the child skills necessary for independent functioning in the world. Many dramas and resistances are traversed in the process of growing up. The appropriate dramas for each stage of human development have been well described by child psychologists. The parents or caregivers may consider themselves successful to the extent that the child enters young adulthood with adequate self confidence, a capacity to function successfully in the world and reasonably high levels of self-responsibility. The child often resists this process every step of the way. She spends time on the plateaus of resistance fighting the growth until they surrender and reach a new level of skill, self-awareness and self-responsibility. Before full development, the child must return over and over to the "home" of the caregiver, to receive the emotional nutrients necessary to continue on the path of maturity. Ideally, there comes a time when the love of the caregivers is experientially known and carried within. The inner hearth has been lit and the fires will always burn. At this point, the child does not have to return home to receive that which she now continually experiences inside. Her heart is open, her love is alive and wherever she goes is "home" because she carries it with her.

So it is with us. Love is our parent, life situations are our lessons and growing up and incorporating the love of the parent is our task. Resistance is the method and surrender and acceptance are the life skills. In this process we develop self confidence, knowledge through experience and become at home in this moment wherever we are in the world.

———◆———

BLAME, PRIDE AND SELF-RESPONSIBILITY

For long periods of time, even over many lifetimes, one can remain in resistance caused by fear. Remaining unseen, resistance can continue indefinitely. Keeping you unaware is the primary method of the ego.

Looking within, the inner dramas of resistance are known at ever more subtle levels. To the degree that one is able to observe these dramas of resistance as a non-participant, awareness and self responsibility expand.

Ego and self responsibility are like oil and water. They cannot be in the same place together. As ego grows, self responsibility diminishes and as self responsibility grows, ego diminishes. As awareness expands, greater self responsibility develops and leaves less and less room for ego to exist and operate.

Ego operates from fear. The ego's fear expresses itself in countless ways but may be said to manifest as either blame or pride. Blame comes from the belief that someone or something has mistreated me in some way, over which I have been powerless. As a result, I have been harmed or threatened. The experience of blame is anger, weakly masking fear. Pride is the feeling stemming from the belief that I have developed exceptional qualities or performed exceptional achievements due to my exceptional abilities and, therefore, I am superior to others. The feeling comes from an arrogance masking fear.

In either of these ego states, "I" is separated from "the other" and the reality of unity is denied. In blame, "I" has denied its own role in the evolution of the particular circumstance. It is a state of low self responsibility. In pride, there is lack of acknowledgment of the contribution of countless other factors outside of the conscious "I" which have helped to lead to the particular achievement or quality development. This lack of acknowledgment is also indicative of low self responsibility. Self responsibility has the obligation to acknowledge reality. In blame, "I" denies its own contributions and in pride, "I" denies the contributions of others. Both states lack awareness and self responsibility and are rooted in fear.

Self responsibility implies the willingness to be aware; awareness of "my" thoughts, feelings, beliefs, actions and words, and awareness of the environment and the other. Self responsibility is the willingness to encounter inner resistance and emotional pain. It is the willingness to acknowledge past errors and false conditioned beliefs within. Self responsibility, therefore, is associated with great courage. It implies the willingness to see and keep seeing even as the layers of painful resistance are encountered and released, the willingness to keep your eyes open to this moment's truth even as the ego rallies ever more forcefully with its fear-based tactics to close your eyes.

As you demonstrate this willingness to see, it becomes easier because of the assistance which comes to you. Previously we have discussed assistance in the forms of the assistance from the unseen ones, the bodily transformative processes which increase receptivity to assistance and the power and reassurance of the direct experience of love. As you persist in maintaining and increasing your awareness, knowledge of the truth, through your direct experience, comes to you in ever increasing amounts. And this truth does set you free. This truth is experienced as the increased power of being in love's light. The inner resistances are cleared one by one, the emotional pain is more easily tolerated and the Self is gradually removed from ego identity. The joy of being in this moment's timeless love-light increases.

—◆—

AS EASY AS WHAT IS, RIGHT NOW

The ego will tell you that all of this is so hard. It views the spiritual transformative process as easy as getting a camel through the eye of a needle. It wants you to give up.

But this process is as easy as turning your attention to the inner and outer reality experiences of this moment. The minute that is done, one is on the path. The practice is to notice resistance encountered and then surrender to the moment's reality. All the rest is given to you; the physical/emotional release, the healing, the assistance from the unseen ones and the ever-increasing joy of love. The river will carry you.

So forgive yourself for the inner realities you encounter. Forgive yourself for your past words and deeds that were destructive or insensitive. Forgive yourself for any judgments you find your ego making upon you. Allow yourself to be exactly where you find yourself, right at this moment.

Love is a river, the great mother, taking you to peace and at-one-ment with all of life. Let her do her job. She does it well and has done so countless times before. She will not fail you as she has never failed the others before you. Your only job is to surrender to her. When you do, she will guide and advise you. You will know.

Be easy. This is not done in a short amount of time. For most, it is not done in a lifetime. However, all who practice attention to the present without attachment will be greatly assisted. There are times wherein the energy of the assistance is great and you are living in such a time now. Take advantage of this special time you now live in and come into the present and see what is with acceptance. Each time you choose to direct your attention to this moment's reality without judgment, you allow the river to take you closer to peace and love's joy. Every step matters. Any and all that you take are cause for celebration. The process goes best when you are not concerned about the finish line. It goes best when you are truly attentive to this moment. The river takes you to the finish line. You will know when you have arrived but then the concept of a finish line will be foreign to you.

———⟫•◆•⟪———

THE DISAPPEARING MAN

At one time, there was a man who sat and watched himself.
He noticed that his legs felt restless and wanted to get up and move.
He just continued to watch.
The restless feelings in his legs lessened and then his legs fell off.

As he continued to watch, he noticed that his nose was itchy.
His mind wanted him to scratch his nose and his arms felt restless.
He just watched.
His arms lost their restless feelings and then fell off
Then his nose disappeared off of his face.

Now he couldn't get up and walk away. He couldn't scratch or smell.
So he just watched.
He noticed that his mind kept thinking word after word.
His tongue felt restless with the urge to speak those words.
But he just watched.
His tongue fell out of his mouth.
His brain fell out of his head through the hole where his nose had been.

Now there were no more words.
Now there was only now.
And in this now he watched his breath.

As he watched, the breath became smaller with longer pauses.
And then there was no breath at all, just one pause.
His lungs vanished.

Now there was no breath and he did not know anything anymore.
So he just kept watching.
But all he could watch was a faint heartbeat.
As he watched this heartbeat it beat faster.
And then it became irregular.
If he had still had his brain, he would have thought he was dying.
But he didn't, so he just watched.
The heartbeat became so fast and irregular that it ceased to be.
And in its place was a high frequency.
This was so fast that it was like a sustained tone.
He kept watching.
He saw that the tone became light.
And this light was all that he was.
He felt joy.
He just kept watching.

At another time, there was a man who knew he was light.
He found himself in a body with arms and legs that could move.
He experienced itching and had a nose that could smell.
He saw that he had a brain that thought words and lungs that
breathed air.
He felt a heartbeat but knew that this was really the sustained tone
of the light.
He just kept watching.
And what he now saw was this body getting up and moving.
He saw it doing things that the light knew as truth.

He saw the eyes recognizing the light coming out of other eyes. He saw the tongue speaking only when prompted by the light. And he saw that these physical gifts he experienced were tools of the light.

BIRTHING THE SELF

By the processes of turning attention inward, surrendering to the experiences encountered and asking for and opening to assistance, the physical form will open up. There is a great energetic drive at this time for human consciousness to grow. In order for this to occur, in most cases, the physical form must also transform to accommodate the greater energies associated with expanded consciousness. Like the ego, the physical form has resistance to change. It wishes to "hold itself together" because the body consciousness, like that of ego, fears death and sees change as death. So, it becomes clear that the body's resistance to physical transformation is based in fear.

The body has assumed chronic armoring postures. The body's tendencies to hold itself certain ways originally began as defensive reactions. Without conscious attention to these defensive reactions, they remained unconscious. That which remains unconscious persists and so these reactions became chronic postural habits.

When the spiritual transformational processes begin, the bodily sensations and postures begin to come into conscious awareness. This change alone catalyzes increased energy into the held postures, encouraging mobilization. When this occurs, the body fears and resists, and the emotions associated with the past circumstances coupled to the original physical defensive reactions begin to rise up. This is why, as discussed earlier, the spiritual transformation process is usually accompanied by strong emotional experiences and grief.

It is not only emotion that occurs with this new awareness. The body expresses its fear and resistance to change through the physical sensations of pain. In ordinary human consciousness, physical pain is feared, resisted and associated with the belief that "something is wrong." Both body and ego-mind resist pain greatly. The ego knows that direct attention to pain is a sign of greater awareness and change. Ego wants consciousness to remain unaware to ensure its continued survival. Therefore, ego encourages the belief that pain is undesirable, threatening and means "something is wrong." When the physical sensations of pain occur, ego mobilizes these beliefs and this in turn leads to attentional distraction from the pain sensations, reactive behaviors to attempt to lessen the pain, increased emotional distress and increased physiological reactions, such as muscular tightening, and changes in blood pressure, heart rate and breathing patterns.

The ego and body consciousness do not want you to continue to be aware of these inner experiences. The spiritual transformation invites you to "just keep watching."

With persistence of attention, the physical pain sensations and emotions intensify and subside. The body eventually mobilizes and increases its capacity to hold and conduct the increased energy. A frequent byproduct of this mobilization is the healing of physical illness. And with the increased energetic capacity of the body, the consciousness expands, leaving less and less room for the old patterns of ego-mind to occupy attention.

Through this process the physical form actually becomes less dense; its matter becomes more conducive of the higher frequency energies. In essence, the form becomes closer in nature to light. Both form and consciousness become expansive. The armoring, both physical and psychological, has lessened or been transcended.

Often, the process has been likened to the birth of a new baby. The labor is filled with fear, resistance, visions of dying and physical pain on the part of both mother and child. At the end of the labor, the mother has expanded into transcendence of the body and the experience of joy. The child has transitioned through the fear of dying and found itself still aware in a mysteriously wonderful new place and, most certainly, not dead.

Spiritual transformation brings us from individual consciousness to unity consciousness, from "I" to "Us", from contraction to expansiveness and from fear of death to new life eternal.

━━◆◆◆━━

THE SPIRITUALITY OF TECHNOLOGY
AND POLITICS

There has never before been a technological expansion in the areas of information processing and communication as is happening at this time. There is movement away from communication through wires towards communication through the atmosphere. The atmosphere has become the template upon which all communication and information can conduct itself. Technology has succeeded in creating an invisible network in the sky and the instruments of transmission and reception. With wireless Internet and cellular telephones, communication and delivery of information can be accomplished with anyone in almost any place. In the near future, one instrument will transmit and receive (in various modalities) all information and communication.

What a wonderful metaphor this is! The rational mind has not yet clearly seen how it is replicating the inherent capacities of expanded human consciousness.

When sufficiently developed, consciousness is capable of perceiving information from anywhere. When sufficiently developed, consciousness is a flawless instrument of reception and transmission. In fact, all information and communication, past, present and future, are eternally available to the proper receptive instrument. Consciousness sufficiently developed has the ability to act like a radio or television and "tune in" to different stations. However, unlike radio or television, its potential stations are not limited.

So it may be said, at this time in the evolution of human consciousness, that there is a drive to manifest in technology the potentials of human consciousness, which are unconsciously sensed in the collective human mind. This is another sign that there is a great energetic drive at this time towards spiritual transformation and expanded consciousness.

As the technology develops, it is clear that many are concerned about "security issues." Many technologies and businesses have been developed in attempt to prevent access to specific communications and information. Ultimately these attempts are doomed as technology will continue to find new ways to access all channels of information.

This dynamic in technology development is a re-creation of the dynamic between the ego-mind and steadily expanding consciousness. Ego-mind strives to hide certain experiences and knowledge from conscious awareness. But because all events, information and communications are essentially "out there," available to all instruments with the proper receptive capacities, ultimately, they cannot be hidden or obscured. All successful "security technologies" will be short lived as technology continues to evolve and expand its receptive capabilities.

The ego-mind, as has been previously discussed, operates by evasion of the present moment and the construction of illusion and untruths. Its motivation is fear for its own survival. The ego-mind simply cannot exist in the light of truth. Expanded consciousness sees ego clearly and, in its vision of light, ego vanishes and the truth is known. As consciousness evolves, the defensive "security technologies" of the ego become less effective until the ego goes "out of business." At that point, technology is less needed because the capacities of expanded consciousness have outpaced and replaced it.

Likewise, the current governing bodies of each country on the Earth are mostly operating from a place of fear for survival. The fear for survival often appears to be a quest for power and control. Other governing bodies manifest their quest for survival by complying and "buddying up" with an ostensibly more powerful country, so as to be protected and cared for by them. The "superpowers" compete for economic predominance and control over resources, producing clashes and egoic defensive behaviors, the most concerning of which are acts of violence. The "lesser" countries become allies in attempt to secure their survival. This is the global stage upon which is played out the ego drama.

This drama is slowly unraveling as human consciousness continues to expand. More and more embodied souls are consciously seeing the increasingly obvious deceits engaged in by the egoic governing bodies. As the truth is known, the lies and true motives become obvious. As a result, the old ploys of egoic governments are working less well than they did in previous times.

The heightened energy of this current time is due to the fact that the collective human consciousness has expanded more than ever before. Individuals in the throws of expanding awareness and the vicissitudes of strain which it places upon their physical, mental and emotional experiences are now frequently confused and may behave unpredictably. Additionally, the resistance the governing bodies are now facing to their old ways is increasing; even if it is not apparent in behavior, the resistance is very real on an energetic level. This resistance is not yet significantly perceived at the level of the five senses. The egoic mind of the governing bodies is beginning to panic and seek more dramatic defensive behaviors, much like a frightened dog, backed into a corner, will begin to growl and bare its teeth more intensely. Unconsciously, the collective ego of the traditional governing bodies knows that its death is imminent. The collective consciousness of the governing bodies has not yet tasted of the non-egoic states of expanded consciousness, but when it does, just as in the individual embodied soul, it will know something other than ego and ego will cease to exist. This will help to lessen the fear.

As consciousness expands more truths become known because the capacity to receive knowledge and truth expands. With this greater awareness and knowledge, human consciousness will learn that the needs of all embodied souls can be met, including those for food and energy. The primary physical needs of all embodied souls can be met without depletion of resources or toxicity to the Earth and its life. There are those who know these methods now and these will become general knowledge soon.

When it is known that there is truly abundance for all and that it is inexhaustible, the old ways of government will cease to exist. Violence will have no place.

And so it can be seen that in the collective body of Earth's peoples regarding technology, communication, government and global relations, the same processes of transformation are occurring as they are in the individual embodied soul who is open to witnessing his or her inner processes. As each individual continues to progress in his or her ability to see and accept without judgment his or her own inner experiences, the evolution of the global human consciousness is furthered.

—◦—

DISTURBING CONFUSION VERSES PEACEFUL UNKNOWING

Passing through a period of confusion is inevitable for most individuals who are open to spiritual transformation. As the ego weakens, the old identity structure begins to dissolve. Consciousness has begun to expand but it is not yet clear who or what one is in this new growing consciousness. The weakening ego still clings to words and explanations and resists its dissolution. It wants to know what all this expanding awareness is and wants to still be your familiar identitiy. Its "wanting to know" is part of its resistance to its own dissolution and your transformation. As consciousness vacillates between opening to direct experience and re-attaching to the old thoughts and beliefs, confusion is inevitable.

There is a difference between disturbing confusion and peaceful unknowing. When there is attachment to the ego, there is disturbance; when dis-identification with the ego is complete, there is peace. The baby in the uncertain labors of the birth canal fears for its survival and anticipates death. The baby's ego is doing all the talking and is unable to be present with the process. After birth, the baby is in the direct experience of being in a new unknown place and the ego-mind is stilled. Existence remains but nothing is known about this new place of being. The baby is filled with the peace of pure being in the absence of the ego.

And so it is with the transformation of the embodied soul. Confusion is the result of the battle of the ego trying to retain its dominance in the increasing power and light of the expanding consciousness, like a shadow trying to retain itself as light is filling the space with greater and greater intensity.

However the confusion presents itself, it may be transformed from disturbance to peaceful unknowing by redirecting attention, in acceptance, to what is occurring in experience at the present moment. This is to be in the experience as opposed to being in commentary about the experience. When this ability has been developed, confusion becomes unknowing. Mastery over attention to remain in present experience is the lesson of the transformational process.

With the development of this mastery comes greater faith and humility, as the embodied soul realizes that he is not so much of an individual, struggling for survival, as he is an aspect of the collective, which is under the direction of the ineffable greater intelligence. Realization of being an aspect of a collective process is a sign of increasing dis-identification with the ego and brings the experience of humility. As the collective process is witnessed by the embodied soul, great faith and gratitude are developed. The miraculous evolutions of the collective process are seen over and over again. The embodied soul realizes that she is a part of this miracle and is filled with joy and gratitude. The miraculous occurrences, observed repetitively, develop deep faith.

The experience of disturbing confusion may be seen as both a sign of progress in the transformational process and an invitation to greater development of mastery of attention upon present experience.

****

These words you have read have been offered to support your transformational process. There are many levels at which this support may occur. The words may speak to the verbal mind offering cognitive understanding of aspects of self experience or the words may trigger memories of concepts previously understood and forgotten.

These words are entrained in the energy of that place within you that knows the felt truth. These words may have heightened the energy of truth within your being and assisted your attention to re-align with that truth. This, in turn, may have resulted in shifts in your somatic and emotional experience. By reading and re-reading these words you may facilitate these shifts in your self experience and thereby find your transformational process quickened. This is their intent. They are words not only to be read and understood but also to be felt and bathed in, as if placing yourself in a strong magnetic field and sensing the polarity of each molecule shifting.

There will be more volumes of writing forthcoming from the same source. Each will have its own specific intent for furthering your transformational process. If this has been helpful, it is hoped that the others will be as well.

It is worth repeating that this is a critical time, a time during which your increasing ability to acknowledge and experience the truth of your being is so greatly needed. In developing these capacities you engage less frequently in the destructive ways of the ego-mind and increasingly radiate the energy of love's truth. When you do, others are affected and changed, even if unconsciously and without visible change. In this way, the Earth and all of its life is healed and transformed. You are supported and honored in any and all attempts you make to know truth. No efforts are without effect.

There is deep gratitude from all beings for your acknowledgement of that place within you that longs for and seeks love's truth. You are not alone.

ABOUT THE AUTHOR

Todd Lyon is a family physician specializing in mind/body medicine. Dr. Lyon frequently presents workshops on mind/body medicine and spirituality. He lives in New Hampshire with his wife, Bonnie, and son, Miles.

Any comments or questions are welcome at
lyonheart_3@msn.com.